# MEN MUST ACT

# MEN MUST ACT

BY LEWIS MUMFORD

HARCOURT, BRACE AND COMPANY    NEW YORK

*Nought can deform the human race*
*Like to the armor's iron brace.*

WILLIAM BLAKE

# CONTENTS

# PREFATORY NOTE

*In the spring of 1938 I published a brief article on the present international situation in The New Republic. Its purpose was to rouse my countrymen from the state of willful optimism in which they confronted world affairs. I urged the need for immediate national action against fascism.*

*This Call to Arms brought forth a painfully specious reply from my friends on The New Republic, whose position it attacked. But it met with a popular response that far outran my expectations: plainly, many thinking people, though their pacifism was even deeper than mine, had already come to the same conclusion: the article had voiced a belief more common than editors and politicians seemed to realize. Since then I have had the turbid pleasure of seeing some of the worst parts of my prophecy fulfilled. And the note of urgency in the original appeal, which seemed to many people unfounded, not to say a little hysterical, in the spring of 1938, has been justified by events: first by the betrayal of democracy at Munich and later by the cold merciless greed for booty and cruelty in the anti-Jewish terrorism in Germany.*

*The purpose of this book is to rally together those who have a firm belief in democracy: this probably includes the greater number of intelligent Americans, representing every shade of economic status and political conviction. For democracy, it is clear now, will not survive by mere passivity or by shamming dead, hoping that fascism will pass by and not notice its ordained victim: nor will democracy survive by self-distrust and harassed surrender. We still have a fighting chance to preserve our Western World against fascist barbarism, but only on one condition*—that we are prepared to fight.

*The United States must be ready to act alone. Once we take the lead both Europe and Latin America, to say nothing of India and China, may find a means of supplying us with allies: meanwhile, the risk and the honor are ours. If fascism is not itself shattered upon meeting in our resistance its first gigantic obstacle, we may nevertheless effectually preserve at least one hemisphere of the world against its triumph.*

*In serving ourselves well, we shall also serve the cause of civilization. And it is for the latter reason that our actions will be gratefully remembered.*

*—L. M.*

# MEN MUST ACT

# 1. THE END OF WISHFUL WAITING

Up to September, 1938, an atmosphere of foggy unreality hung over current discussions of peace: despite a succession of fascist barbarities since 1931, it still persisted. During the past twenty years many proposals had been made to keep war from descending upon the world: by 1938, these proposals were based upon a world that no longer existed. The proposals were dated 1938: but the premises remained those of 1928. Accommodation, adjustment, amelioration, justice—these were the humane concepts of a pre-fascist world. They were no longer the key to establishing a well-ordered peace for one sharp reason: the fascist states of Germany and Italy rejected the very aim of rational co-operation. And their actions in Spain threw a light upon their glib promises everywhere else.

This failure to keep up with actual events has proved almost as fatal as the events themselves. Though the catastrophic "peace" of Munich has done much to open the eyes of Americans, they still see the whole problem of democracy's survival in too narrow a framework. Many peace-loving people are still trying to persuade themselves that fascism is not what it seems and that fascists do not mean to do the things they actually do. These advocates of a pre-fascist peace regard as enemies, less the fascists themselves, than those who have the moral convictions to oppose them. So afraid are these groups of possibly bringing on war, that despite the horrors that accumulate in Europe, they oppose armed resistance to fascism as itself a species of fascism. With the best motives in the world, they nevertheless play into the fascists' hands.

In this attitude the absolute pacifist gets re-enforcement from the ordinary citizen; for the natural reaction of every decent soul from the horrible possibility of war is to retreat from it. With no little reason the ordinary citizen believes that munitions makers are war-mongers: did they not in fact adroitly wreck successive disarmament conferences? Those who have been interested in the promotion of armament during the past have not, in general, been those who were interested in peace, in social justice, in political equity: on the contrary, they have often been those who openly or secretly worked for the dictator-

4

ship of capital, and the rights of strong nations to browbeat and exploit the weaker peoples of the world.

In the past, munitions makers, imperialists, patrioteers have always exalted the need for military force: their economic interests coincided visibly with their duties as citizens, as they conceived them. No peaceful citizen wants to be caught in such company. Preparation for war, everyone is shrewd enough to see now, is not ordinarily a hopeful means of ensuring peace. Why, therefore, should we take steps that may only bring war that much nearer?

To make their tacit alliance with fascism easier, the absolute pacifists have, until recently, adopted an optimistic attitude toward fascism itself. They have treated fascism as if it were entirely a product of the villainous political and economic conditions introduced by the Treaty of Versailles. This is a partial, and therefore essentially false, interpretation of both the doctrine and the situation in which it has flourished. They have fancied that if the original political "causes" of fascism were removed, the totalitarian state itself would gracefully vanish. Surely, they have said to themselves, turning away from the latest fascist barbarity in the morning paper, the world cannot be as bad as that: what becomes of the notion of prog-

5

ress? Or if the world is so bad, and if men and women have turned their backs on their own humanity, it cannot long remain so.

Fascism, indeed, has profited by two facts: one is that every country has in some degree its own symptoms of fascist pathology: hence a guilty conscience. Likewise every country has reactionary groups that, sooner than reduce their own status, are ready to surrender their country to fascism: witness the actions of the French bankers and the Comité des Forges. And the other reason is that its extremes of cruelty, violence, and irrationality are humanly incredible: and so people, at least until the bestial outbreak against the defenseless Jews took place in Germany in November, 1938, have doubted their existence, against undeniable evidence, indeed against the boastful declarations of the fascists themselves.

Too long has a meek acquiescence greeted the spread of fascism. This moral paralysis accounts for both its internal and its foreign successes far more than the dynamic qualities of its leadership. The very ruthlessness of fascism has been in proportion to the lack of opposition it has encountered: its special forms of heroism rise to their truly fascist height only when fascist gangs have the opportunity to kick prostrate

6

old Jews, bait priests, or rain bombs on children. But thanks to the continuance of these superb displays of fascist courage, the world has now apparently crossed the threshold of tolerance: even Mr. Chamberlain has not been able to approve openly of the acts of his fascist overlord, with whom he perpetrated the hypocritical pretense of "peace in our time."

By now we have apparently reached the end of a period: the period of wishful waiting. The longer we wait, it is now plain, the worse the situation grows. The international night darkens. The chill of a merciless reality by now has penetrated the meekest spines. Our American democracy can no longer join in the European retreat. Intelligently, manfully, we must face the world into which our children are now being born—a hideous world in contrast to that which existed, in all its contradictions, its weaknesses, its imperfections, in 1914.

To close one's eyes to the present international situation because the remedy for it is a difficult and hazardous one is a form of self-indulgence that the honest critical mind must not permit itself. Sheer inertia still makes people minimize the danger: in a recent storm people stayed in their houses on Long

Island, convinced that the incoming waves would not reach them, because the tides had never climbed so high before. Too late, many unfortunates discovered that the rules that held in the past did not apply to this particular tornado: the waves swept in.

The one kind of *ism* that no intelligent man should hold today is optimism. There has probably not been a time when the outlook for humanity was so black since the fourteenth century, the century of the Black Death. To fancy that fascism will sweep over the world and leave America untouched, merely because we wish to be let alone, is to imagine that we will be protected by a miracle. Nor may one still hope that time will by itself alter the present situation. Time changes nothing: *men must act*. Hoping for the best, we must still prepare for the worst. To face the future in any other spirit is to invite destruction.

# 2. THE CLAIMS OF FASCISM

As an historic fact, fascism first emerged as a political party: an opportunist catchall of revolutionary and reactionary doctrines. In the course of events, first in Italy, later in Germany, this party took possession of the government and displaced the existing parties that had debated and argued and maneuvered in parliament. The instruments of its overthrow were, first, individual bands of rowdies who ganged up on opposition groups, assaulted them, dosed them with castor oil: the seal of its success was the use of state police and soldiers to give to the method of terrorism official sanction and more widespread effectiveness.

Fascism went back to the earlier method of administration that had preceded constitutional government. It relied on despotic rule: one man, one party, one clique. This is the basis of its claim to be "youthful" and "modern." By resorting to military force as the main sanction of government, fascism placed its entire population under martial law: by attempting to be self-sufficient in the supply of goods, it reduced Italy

9

and Germany to their present condition: a self-imposed state of siege. No one understands the first principle of fascism until he recognizes that through these methods war has been normalized, in Italy and Germany, into a permanent state of life. Under such conditions it is peace, not war, that constitutes a threat to the life of the "state"—that is, of the fascist party and its dictator.

To hope, with Mr. Chamberlain's maudlin persistence, that the fascist countries will at least make a "gesture" to signify that they desire peace, betrays a fundamental misunderstanding of fascism. Why should they contradict themselves? Why should they renounce the source of their power? Only wilful political illiterates—who can neither read the fascist leaders' speeches, nor yet the handwriting on the wall —can persuade themselves that fascists may have a "change of heart." Fascists cannot afford luxuries— not even the British luxury of hypocrisy.

In a psychological sense, fascism's youthfulness is indeed its most outstanding characteristic: but hardly in the sense that fascists pride themselves on the fact. Plainly, fascism carries into the conduct of adult men and women the infantile illusions of power that the baby first feels in its crib when, by bawling loudly, it achieves magical results: the light in its room is turned on or its diaper is changed without further effort on the part of the child. In the course of grow-ing up, that untrammeled sense of power meets the resistance of hard facts and the needs of other men: but the desire to achieve this magical obedience does not easily depart. Those who cannot achieve wealth by their own exertions imagine themselves a moving picture magnate: those who cannot achieve power, transfer their wishes to their leader.

By his idolatrous worship of the leader the fascist achieves another infantile wish: he not merely has a vicarious sense of power, but he is comforted by the protecting image of the Father. Like a boastful six-year-old, he believes that his father is stronger than Johnny's father; his father is smarter, too; his father can shoot straighter, too; his father can punch any-one's nose if he likes. It is not the "youth" of fas-cism that makes it attractive but its infantilism. As a political cult, it is a means of keeping mankind in diapers.

Now the claim to originality that fascism makes today does not rest upon its doctrine of single party government; nor does it rest upon the concentration of power into the hands of the leader. Both these are

11

ancient devices of government, so full of weaknesses and intolerable faults that at the first crack in the wall of absolute rule the whole structure is always in danger of tumbling down. Against domestic despotism, with all its irresponsibility and tyrannous whimsy, the revolutions that took place in England, the United States, and France in the seventeenth and eighteenth centuries were fought: well fought.

Plainly, what is wrong with despotism is not the fact of power but the way in which it is exercised. In any country there may be moments of crisis in which a forceful display of authority is preferable to continued chaos. Very wisely, the founders of the American constitution recognized such moments, and made provision for the concentration of power in the hands of the chief executive, with a fullness that rivals that of any self-appointed dictator. But behind such temporary mobilizations is a safeguard: when the crisis is over, authority returns to the several organs from which the executive derives his power. If he has acted in a fashion that denies his oath of office to uphold the constitution, he may be impeached. In short, a mechanism exists for restoring the normal processes of government: for permitting division, dissent, the challenge of contrary opinion.

During the World War, Woodrow Wilson exercised as much power as does Hitler or Mussolini. Because of his undoubted world popularity during the six months that preceded the signing of the Versailles Treaty, he was the most powerful ruler in the world. But that fact did not convert his rule in America into a dictatorship: far from it. Though officers in Wilson's war cabinet instituted the most flagrant violations of constitutional rights even after the war was over, the practices of republican government did not for that reason finally disappear. Neither Wilson, nor his soldierly and somewhat embittered rival, General Leonard Wood, led a march on Washington to overthrow what remained of constitutional government. Because the United States, with a hundred and fifty years' experience behind it, is a seasoned republican government, we reverted once more to rule by law: government with the consent of the governed.

The same conclusions apply to the economic crisis of 1933 when Franklin Roosevelt, very properly in the circumstances, secured a concentration of responsibility, in order to act swiftly in a series of emergencies. To confuse his actions with those of a dictator is something that even the most violent reactionaries hesitated to do as long as their possessions and their

13

lives were threatened by economic chaos. What democracy fears is not power but irresponsibility. The vice of fascism, in contrast, is that it combines a maximum capacity for abusing power with a maximum denial of responsibility. Theoretically the dictator cannot be impeached: practically he cannot even be assassinated.

What is novel, then, about fascism is not its permanent concentration of political power, but the form that this power has taken. Fascism comes into existence by reason of a crisis: it continues in existence by creating a series of crises, or at least by maintaining the illusion that some other party, some other group, or some other country is about to bring a crisis into existence. Dr. Max Lerner has well called fascism "crisis government." As far as results go, one need not inquire too closely whether the crisis is only an imagined one or whether it is a real one: the existence of vast debts, a growing army of unemployed, a harassed, dissatisfied middle class; or some combination of real difficulties and imaginary terrors.

The crisis is the source of fascism's power: the fascists must prolong the crisis in order to maintain their power. If peace and security and civil well-being were in their possession, they would have to renounce

14

them. One needs no better proof of this fact than the behavior of the German Nazis after Hitler had dictated the "peace" of Munich. A government that exists by terrorism is forever hounded by a baleful shadow —the shadow of peace. This is one gift that fascism cannot use to its own advantage. Did not Hitler almost ruin Mr. Chamberlain's deft plan for generously giving Czechoslovakia's territories and industries to Germany by demanding the right to seize them for himself? He was forced to risk war in order to turn the patron's gift into the "conqueror's" booty.

## 3. CIVILIZATION'S GORDIAN KNOT

The violence and ruthlessness of fascism differ from occasional outbreaks of these qualities in civilized countries by one chief mark: their government is inconceivable without it. In strict truth, fascism is government by martial law: the fundamental basis of its rule is, so to say, the riot act. That the fascists themselves provoke the riot, in order to gain the assent of the passive majority to their hideous measures of suppression, there is plenty of evidence to prove, both in Italy and in Germany. What is important to realize is that the violence of fascism is not accidental. Without violence, fascism could neither exist nor perpetuate itself: without the cowardly aid of the more civilized nations of the world, fascism could neither extend its conquests nor even stabilize its domestic regime.

Unqualified brutality produces an inevitable reaction: unqualified fear. In this state, only one thought possesses the victim: that of avoiding any act that would provoke the unscrupulous agents of terror.

Mussolini discovered the dynamics of fear after the Matteotti assassination; Hitler exploited it from the moment he was thrust into power. But government by fear is like x-ray therapy; if prolonged beyond the minimum dosage it not merely destroys the tissues of political society but burns the operator. The more a state relies on fear, the more it becomes the victim of its own nightmares.

When fear seizes a people, murder and suicide become the most grateful means of solving their main problem—how to find a way out. Fascism resorts to the first and hopes that its intended victim will accept the second. The murder and the suicide are both real and figurative: that is, the opponents of fascism are actually killed in the process of achieving totalitarian unanimity; and, in addition, the very process of fascist rule assaults the spirit as violently as it attacks the bodies of men. Those who accept life under fascism enjoy only such aspects of life as submit wholly to external regimentation. The superstitions of race and nationality, the myth of the leader's godhood, the lies of the propagandist bureau, the constant diet of malice, brutality, and terrorism—the daily dosage of these poisons, without benefit of antidotes, is the price of continued existence under a fascist regime.

17

Humanly speaking, the process is murder and the willing acceptance of it is suicide. For real men and women, capable of exercising all the organs and capacities of a complete human being, life in a fascist country is at best a long period of confinement in a prison: a topsy-turvy prison in which the real criminals pass sentence and stand guard, while innocent men are branded with the epithets of disgrace. One has only to talk with those who had been trapped by fascism and who finally escaped from their native country to realize that the supreme feeling that energizes them when they reach the United States is not merely a sense of freedom—the ability to talk without suspecting the presence of spies and to think and write freely without fearing, at each ring of the doorbell, a visit of the secret police—but is much more than this. It is the feeling they have of actually recovering their manhood: the sense of spiritual castration disappears.

The reliance upon force and military assault as a source of political authority one may call the fallacy of Alexander—the pattern and image of all modern dictators from Napoleon onward. Everyone knows the famous exploit of Alexander with the Gordian knot. When one first hears that story, as a little child, one says: What a clever man Alexander was and how stupid all the fumblers with the knot must have been. But as one ponders its meaning, one reverses one's first judgment: one respects the patient fumblers and one laughs instead at the arrogant youth who, in his hot impatience, solved the problem by doing away with the very elements that made it a problem: namely, the nature of the knot and the continuity of the cord itself. Any fool can showily solve the real problems of political power by martial law: but only a fool would mistake that process for government.

Obedience by terrorism: unity by suppression: singleness of purpose by defrauding society of every purpose except that of the dictators—this is too easy. It is only in insane asylums or under dictatorships that life is ever as simple as that. The whole problem of political society consists in achieving order out of a multitude of conflicting interests: in achieving common purposes without annihilating individual energies and aptitudes and designs. On fascist principles, one might reasonably try to win a football game by poisoning the opposing team before the game began. On those terms, winning would be easy but the meaning of victory would disappear.

To take our parable of the knot further, civilization

19

is composed of many strands: like a cable, as opposed to a wire of the same dimensions, the twisting together of these different strands increases not merely its flexibility but its strength. There are strands of economic interest, strands of racial and national and family inheritance, strands of religious belief, strands of different grades of psychological experience and education. Each generation finds itself confronted with a Gordian knot that must be untied. The press of events, the impact of economic interests, the choices of personality, shifts in power and culture, change the nature of the knot. Now it is the need for free government; now it is the desire to abolish slavery; now it is the control of overbearing monopolies; now it is the radical re-distribution of the annual income and the raising of the real standard of living: economic security. The knots are various; they are inescapable. But the prime political condition of untying the knot is this: the rope itself shall be unharmed. To cleave the Gordian knot with a sword is to destroy the very values of civilization: that is, the capacity to hold together many strands of its inheritance, to twist them into strong ropes, to bind them together into new knots, to untie the old knots when conditions change again.

20

This task is an unending one; no generation finishes it; and in a sense, no knot is ever finally untied: as Whitman says, we but reach our goal to pass beyond it. The patient fumbling hand is however a better image of the task than the slashing sword: for though the sword may quickly undo the knot it leaves the difficulties symbolized by the knot unsolved. If government by crisis is one name for fascism, shortcut government is another. Dictatorships seek by fiat to achieve results that democratic governments have learned to seek by the longer, more tedious route of explanation, discussion, argument, resolution of differences, consent, and finally rational collective action.

The immediate result under the democratic method comes more slowly: the final effect is probably more lasting, precisely because the differences have been ironed out beforehand. The very speed and absolutism of fascism means that it never has the advantage of second thoughts. In the region where I live the country people sometimes say: "Ain't that something to think about all day and never do." The fascists would not understand this prudent folksay. Their habit is to do something all day and never think about it.

Terrorism: repression: salutary violence: collective

21

blackmail: mob assemblages: oratorical masturbation: monstrous parades—these are the main weapons whereby fascist dictatorships achieve power and remain in possession of it. But the very contents of political life is changed by this process: a nation that spends twenty-four hours a day in a Nazi uniform is like an individual who spends twenty-four hours a day looking into his own mirror. Eighty million little Hitlers have only the strength, the intelligence, and the cunning of a single man: they may conceive themselves as mystically participating in the rites of godhood: actually the completeness of their unanimity marks the extent of their feebleness. The more the dictatorship succeeds in stamping the leader's image upon every aspect of life, the more impoverished the country becomes. After a while, the unanimity, which was at first a bluff and a lie, becomes more or less of a fact. Such power devitalizes itself by its very success.

For the fact is that variety and conflict and dissent are weaknesses only to those who are too lacking in fortitude to undergo the normal processes of life: violent coercion is the quack's shortcut to political health. Hence fascism is essentially an invention of the weak and the neurotic: a reputed coward like

Mussolini, a paralyzed hysteric like Hitler, attempt to overcompensate for their obvious weaknesses by mounting the very horses that have unseated them: they pick up thousands of followers who are equally degraded by self-contempt, equally smitten by self-distrust, equally tormented by their own sense of inferiority. By the high, exacting standards of a humane culture, these people are, in their own consciousness, failures. To recover their sense of self-respect they had the alternative of effectually transforming themselves or of rejecting the standards of civilization. The first alternative might have required the services of a psychiatrist. Instead they erected their disordered psychological state as a measuring rod for civilization. By drawing together millions of fellow-sufferers, they normalized their neurosis.

# 4. THE BARBARIAN ALTERNATIVE

Behind fascism's moldy resurrection of despotism is something far more sinister: its deliberate appeal to the raw primitive and its positive glorification of barbarism. As a political system, it might be regarded as an error of politically undeveloped countries, such as Italy and Germany historically were and are: now more than ever. But as a system of ideas its capacity for mischief is of a much wider order.

To understand the growing popularity of barbarism, one must indeed understand the weaknesses of our contemporary civilization. During the last two centuries Western Civilization, developing too quickly, too ruthlessly, under the tutelage of the inventor and the capitalist, has often demanded sacrifices out of all proportion to its visible benefits. In precisely those points where it has achieved a certain equilibrium, its results have proved unsatisfactory in many respects to the common man. Each day brings with it a burdensome routine: the anxious efforts at punctuality, the necessity for speed and machinelike efficiency in production, the need to suppress personal reactions in an impersonal process, the painful sense of universal insecurity and impotence that an ill-organized, socially irresponsible system of production has brought about—all these things have created a deep malaise. Automatism and compulsion become pervasive: the human personality becomes dwarfed. Totalitarian dictatorships, in one sense, only mobilize this sense of defeat and direct it to their own ends: an attack on civilization itself.

There are two ways of meeting this situation. One is to alter both the goals of living and the means employed: to put social service above private profit and collective advantage above individual power; to shorten the number of monotonous hours; to provide variety in work and autonomy in every department where it can be re-introduced; to enlist an active and intelligent co-operation within the office and the factory and the farmstead instead of permitting the absolute dictatorship of the financial system: in short, to substitute co-operative processes for the parasitic and predatory ones that have so long dominated machine industry and its subsidiary occupations. All these means involve drastic changes in the existing institutions: particularly in mitigating the absolutism

25

of private property and in redistributing the annual income of the community. They also involve far deeper psychological understanding, far more expert administrative and legislative skill, than either business or politics can yet show today.

The fascist means of meeting this situation is to accept the automatisms that capitalist industry has created: to accept them and make them more universal. Instead of less regimentation, a greater amount of it; instead of higher wages and shorter hours, lower wages and longer hours; instead of a larger proportion of consumer's goods and less instrumental goods, just the reverse of this: substituting guns for butter, battleships for bread, bombproof shelters and trenches for housing. In short, they double the bitter dose in order to make it more palatable, as a person sometimes presses against an aching tooth in order to relieve the pain.

Now the flouting of man's unconscious drives and his warmest emotional impulses cannot without danger continue indefinitely. The desire for communion with nature will not be satisfied long by Sportsman's Shows and by automobile drives on mountain crestlines; the desire for adventure will not be sated by reports of murder and sudden death in the daily newspaper; even sport, which serves as an outlet for many aggressive impulses, cannot serve its function as long as most of its participants are mere spectators.

Beyond these obvious needs are even deeper subjective impulses: the desire for a life that shall be meaningful and purposive, not blank and sterile, that shall be formative and creative, not completely subservient to outward circumstances. Subjective needs are no less imperious than external conditions. When the industrial routine and mechanical standards of achievement deny these needs, they dam up the very flow of life: this creates dangerous pressures within. The repressed ego, thwarted, humiliated, debased, will seek an outlet through a lower activity if the higher channels are blocked.

There is a civilized way of giving depth and dignity and sustained outward expression to man's subjective impulses; but most people have no access to this discipline except through the ancient rituals of the Church. And the intellectual culture of our time has been too remote from the masses either to recognize their needs or to serve them satisfactorily; while the continued otherworldliness of the Church's doctrines has made its counsels suspect to the mass of

27

men who want a heaven closer at hand. In this state of acute frustration, men seek by magical rites to achieve immediate power: out of their impotence they project an omnipotent Leader. And in order to achieve expression of their now maimed impulses, they collectively follow the example of Captain Ahab in "Moby Dick": blindly, desperately, they seek revenge. Here is where fascism steps in to aid them.

Now who shall be the butt of this revenge? Immediately, real people, Jews, Communists, Catholics, pacifists, orthodox Protestants, who may be seized and terrorized: whose homes may be looted, whose shops may be destroyed, whose churches and synagogues may be fired or stoned, whose bodies may be maltreated. But eventually a greater enemy becomes the object of revenge: civilization itself. The fact that it is the source of all that makes us properly human is forgotten: or rather, that is precisely what lays it open to attack.

For the fascist deliberately glorifies the sub-human: he favors all that helps behavior to return to a baser level of emotion and feeling. This second solution leaves our entire mechanical apparatus momentarily intact: indeed, its armaments are needed in order to make more effective the fascist's deliberate mobilizations of ferocity. Eventually, however, fascism must destroy not alone our highest mechanical and scientific achievements, but the more general sense of order upon which they are founded. In this relapse into the primitive the ultimate defeat and degradation become universal. Not merely does the worker become an industrial serf: throughout society, servile institutions replace civil ones.

Fascism distinguishes itself from earlier forms of despotism, which grew out of more primitive means of aggression, in that it proudly associates itself with this deliberate return to barbarism. Whatever coherence fascism has as a system of ideas derives from the cult of barbarism: that is the point where its brutal practices take on an "ideal" tinge. The marks of fascism, as a system of ideas, may be briefly summed up:

FIRST: *glorification of war:* war as the permanent state of mankind and as the perfect medium for fascist barbarism. The belief in war as an attribute of all virile nations is a primary mark of fascism: it is bellicose even when it is chicken-hearted. Any attempt to lessen the possibility of war is from this standpoint a confession of weakness and futility. In practice, war is conceived as a one-sided method of butchering the weak and looting the submissive: hence the display of arms and the belching of fascist eloquence sufficiently satisfies the fascist demand for martial glory, provided the victim is inclined to purchase "peace" by surrender. But war remains the basis of the state: the drilling of the soldier is a holy duty; for the aim is to make a whole population obedient to command, like an army. Life for the fascist reaches its highest point on the battlefield: or, failing that, on the parade ground.

SECOND: *contempt for the physically weak.* Whereas Christianity made the meek, the humble, and the weak the very basis of its system of love and charity, fascism does just the opposite: the weak are either to be exterminated or to be used as the objects of sadistic sport. While Christianity elevated to a high place the domestic virtues, fascism has mercy only for the strong and pity only for the more powerful: the fascist prides himself upon being a carnivore, as Spengler proclaimed, though in actual fact man is the chief of the domestic animals: his first achievement in domestication was himself. Politically speaking, all minorities are in the class of the physically weak: hence they are detestable to fascists except as objects of aggression.

30

THIRD: *contempt for science and objectivity.* Because fascism is based upon a series of shabby myths and pseudo-scientific pretensions which would disgrace the intelligence of a well-educated modern schoolboy, it must reject science. By what rational means could it possibly establish the existence of an Aryan race, the divinity of a Duce or a Fuehrer, the purity of national blood, and the universal degeneracy of Jews, Liberals, Socialists, Catholics, and all non-white races except those distinguished Aryans, the Japanese?

Objective science naturally reduces these imbecile claims to ashes: hence science must submit to official rape before it may be pursued in fascist countries. For science is a means of arriving at results by methods of measuring and testing that all other men in full possession of their senses may, with similar preparation and discipline, follow. It leads to action on the basis of proved knowledge, rather than action on the basis of mere dream-fantasy and irrational impulse. Fascism, on the other hand, rests upon an addled subjectivity: what the leader desires is real: what he believes is true: what he anathematizes is heresy. These fiat truths bring about a debasement of the entire intellectual currency.

Since science requires patient effort and keen discipline and long training, fascism provides a cheap vulgar substitute: with the sword of its obsessive dogmas it cuts the Gordian knot of knowledge, too. The operation is quite as successful here as in political life: that is, it extirpates real knowledge and leaves the minds of its docile pupils open to whatever propagandist concoctions the needs of the prevailing crisis may dictate. Italy's sudden discovery of its Aryanism was timed exquisitely to harmonize with the need for strengthening the Rome-Berlin axis. To see things as they really are—which is another phrase for objectivity—is the last thing that a dictator would have happen: for it is the danger of all dangers to the system of illusions upon which his power is established.

FOURTH: *hatred for democracy*. The chief source of this hate I will go into later: here it is enough to record that the hate is a double-faced one; for despotism is, as Aristotle knew, a bastard child of democracy. Even now, through its absurd plebiscites, fascism occasionally goes through the motions of casting a ballot, though the population has lost the right of election. By playing upon the more infantile illusions of the masses the fascists hope to stave off the development of popular groups that will challenge

32

their power. But democracy, in the sense of responsible popular control and popular initiative, is the chief obstacle to smooth fascist leadership. Hence fascism uses democracy's own healthy skepticism as to its weaknesses and mistakes as a weapon for undermining its own self-confidence. The essential difference between democracy and fascism, as concerns mistakes, is that fascist governments have the privilege of covering them up. *By definition,* the leader can make no mistakes.

FIFTH: *hatred for civilization.* If fraud is better than honesty, if propagandist lies are better than objective truth, if arbitrary force is better than rational persuasion, if brutality is preferable to mercy, if aggressive assault is preferable to co-operative understanding, if illusions are better than scientific facts, if war and destruction are better than peace and culture—then barbarism is better than civilization, and fascism, as the systematic inculcation of barbarism, is a grand gift to humanity. Fascism, both by its proclamations and its actions, leaves no doubt as to its source or its preference. Though whatever energy fascism exhibits is due to the fact that it still can live parasitically upon the remains of civilization, its own specific contributions are barbaric ones.

Fascist civilization, in short, is a contradiction in terms. We have not yet witnessed a fascist civilization; and we are not likely to do so; for if civilization comes again in Germany and Italy, it will be as the result of overthrowing fascism. What the visitor is usually shown as fascist achievements are the results of the common culture that fascism has inherited and not yet completely despoiled. What will finally emerge, if fascism continues to prevail in Europe, will be a system of barbarism: its stunted, emasculated minds: its grandiose emptiness: its formalized savagery. Fifty thousand hoarse voices shouting *Sieg Heil:* that is fascist music. A parade ground for a hundred thousand goose-steppers, drilled into flat-footedness: that is Nazi civic art.

Hatred for civilization is a hatred for mind, sensibility, or feeling that shows any degree of complexity or exhibits any wider connections with the world outside the crude parochial ego. What the fascist calls order is the order of Procrustes: the systematic elimination of the differences and variations which give to a true culture its inexhaustible variety: the fascist prefers to cut off the leg that will not fit the fascist bed.

SIXTH—and finally: *fascism crowns its imbecilities, its superstitions, and its hatreds with one mastering obsession: delight in physical cruelty.* This is one of the true stigmata of fascism. From the castor-oil treatment first administered by the Italian fascists to the merciless beating and gougings and maimings practiced in Nazi concentration camps and prisons, a strong bent toward sadism is even more characteristic of fascism than sheer aggression: for aggression against an equal always carries with it the possibility of incurring suffering as well as inflicting it: fascists do not attack equals. For nations to qualify as fascist victims they must be small enough to be stamped on and smeared with blood without risk to the fascist aggressor (hero).

Make no doubt of it: barbarism is the easy way of life. One has only to let go: to shout when one is angry, hate aggressively when one is frustrated, destroy when one is puzzled. In return for this letting go, one must take orders: but this, in fact, is another kind of letting go—permitting the leader to do one's thinking and to give the answer to questions that would otherwise have involved thought, conflict, responsible decision. Fascism therefore calls to those who have not yet emerged from infantilism and to those who would like speedily to return to it: it is the way of regression. It is a political system that appeals to rapacious industrialists, disappointed political arrivistes, and frustrated mediocrities. Civilization on the other hand is the hard way: it is the way of disciplined growth: it involves efforts beside which the fascists' repetitious drills and routines, however strenuous, are mere child's play. The relapse into barbarism is a recurrent temptation. Only *men* can resist it.

# 5. DEMOCRACY EQUALS CIVILIZATION

Democracy is not a system of government but a way of life: it is consistent with many systems of government. A democracy may be governed by lot, as in Athens; it may be governed by elected representatives. Its executive power may be diffused, as in pre-Civil War United States; or it may be concentrated, as took place afterwards. It may be militantly national, as in France during the revolution of 1789; or it may be free from class exploitation and war, as Iceland seems once to have been. It may rest upon a written constitution, as in the United States, or it may be governed by traditions, precedents, blind habits, many only partly formulated, as in Great Britain. It may be agrarian or capitalistic or socialistic.

Two things chiefly characterize the democratic method. The first is the participation and consent of the governed: not merely that passive acquiescence without which no government can long remain in power, but the active consent, at intervals of consultation, after discussion and free argument. Consent presupposes two other conditions: free inquiry and free choice.

In other words, democracy is the substitution of education for irrational coercion: this rests not so much upon the institution of schools as upon the search for a common ground in every situation that involves conflict: an effort to substitute intelligence for brute force, law for caprice or prejudice, rational morality for blind *mores*. Democracy, just because it cannot afford to sacrifice freedom in order to arrive at quick decisions, does not prosper in a crisis: it must take its time. The accommodation of different points of view, the harmonization of strong antagonisms, the resolution of conflicts—these things are the essence of the democratic method.

The second principle is respect for the human individual and for the endless forms which individuality takes through group expression and counter-expression. Not merely has every man, ultimately, a claim to be understood and a right to be heard: but every shade and variety of belief, opinion, doctrine, must be represented if an issue is to be soundly defined or rationally decided. A democracy that denies this, as Athens did in the time of Socrates, has already opened its grave. Unity by inclusion rather than unity by suppression, extirpation, exclusion, is the principle of democracy.

In democracy's very looseness and lack of rigidity lies its main strength: it must create a multitude of autonomous centers in order not to rely upon the authority of a single one. The diffusion of intelligence and responsibility is the very test of a democracy.

No democracy can be run by dupes, robots, or automatons. The critical problem for every democracy lies in the process of education; and the upshot of its demand for intelligence and for emotional balance is to make education a continuous function of life. Men have better knowledge of their immediate neighborhood than of the great world beyond them; they know their own occupations and problems better than those of their neighbors: hence democracy has flourished better in a small-scale society, as in Jefferson's time, or in the equally small-scale society of the medieval free city, than it has done later in more complicated and impersonal economic regimes.

The problem of improving the working arrangements of democracy has only been opened up: no one can pretend that the sporadic canvassing of opinion that now takes place under parliamentary government is an effective answer to the problem of modern political control. The fact is that the political system cannot be effectively democratic until a similar diffusion of power and responsibility takes place in our economic system. People who spend their hours accepting decisions made for them elsewhere, and then spend the rest of their waking day under the spell of advertisers, salesmen, and radio announcers, who attempt to reduce to automatism all their free functions—these people cannot effectively control their political life. Self-government, for a democracy, is both an individual and a collective need.

But our democratic polity is not washed up: it has hardly been launched. *With the promise of leisure that modern invention has opened up and wise administration will make possible, the opportunity for a fully democratic society of wide range is only just coming into existence.* Politics, the organization and administration of common activities, is a difficult and fascinating game: a game that democratic society will not willingly permit to remain in the hands of mediocre professionals. Every trade union, every cooperative society, every neighborhood association, is a training ground for the more complicated problems of collective government.

What we have now by way of political democracy

is a very partial thing. In the past it has been frustrated by two-fisted robber barons who practiced a despotism in industry that set an example for the fuller absolutism of the fascists: likewise this democracy was hedged in deliberately by constitutional arrangements that subordinated the common welfare to property rights, and it was challenged by the local absolutism of political bosses and financial bosses who took advantage of the very looseness of the democratic structure to violate its principles. The Boss of American political life is indeed the prototype of Il Duce or der Fuehrer: but without the halo, the hooey, or the hallucinations. As Boss, he has merely human dimensions.

Unfinished and half-way democracy still is: no doubt of that. The necessity to concentrate responsibility, to employ high technical ability, to supplant the leadership of affable mediocrities afflicted with a gift of gab, to alter the existing structure of our economic life so as to spread purchasing power more equitably and create human security—these tasks, and many others, lie before us. But although political democracy is still a spindly plant, not a tree big enough to give protection, democracy as a way of life is infinitely stronger and broader than its political shadow.

As a way of life democracy has now become synonymous with civilization: it is democracy, rather than communism, that is the real alternative to fascist barbarism. Evils of all sorts exist in democratic countries: exhibitions of arbitrary power, class exploitation, local outbreaks of collective sadism, like the sporadic lynching of Negroes in the South. But, unlike fascism, democracy is not based upon the existence of these evils; nor does it exult in them and proclaim them to be the new virtues.

So it comes to this. There is nothing that civilized men anywhere have developed and cherished that a democratic polity, as such, rejects: rather, it gives free play to all the forces and institutions and ideas that have led to the humanization of man: if fascism has contributed anything to the sum total of human knowledge or human development, democracy must be ready to include these lessons in its own synthesis.

Fascism, on the other hand, distrusts civilization as such: under the impact of its monstrous collective demonism, it deliberately, as a necessary part of its mechanism of defense, tramples upon the humaner virtues.

42

To measure the unbridgeable gulf between fascist barbarism and democratic civilization becomes, therefore, the first duty of every intelligent citizen today. And a heavy onus rests on those who would minimize this gulf: under the guise of cool sobriety and even-handed justice they place their weight on the side of those whose first effort will be to disturb this sobriety and upset this justice. One willingly grants that fascism is an exaggeration of tendencies that now exist everywhere: its demented cult of patriotism, its raucous nationalism, its militarism, its absolutism, even its systematic sadism can be matched with similar phenomena in every other country. One admits this freely; just as every honest person will admit in his own heart impulses which, if they became fixed, obsessive, overstressed, would lead him to the gallows or the insane asylum.

But what does this admission prove? There are liberals, like Mr. Bruce Bliven, for example, who appear unctuously to think that these facts remove the moral right of a citizen in a democracy to fight foreign fascism. On the contrary: the existence of fascist methods, fascist doctrines, fascist organizations in America does not lessen our responsibility to resist the outside assault: it increases it. For unless we resist it, the poisonous elements that confessedly exist in what are now small and controllable quantities may ultimately paralyze our whole body politic. The Ku Klux Klan and its Kleagles once crazily threatened our American polity as the Nazis threatened Republican Germany: fortunately, we had enough mental health to laugh the menace out of existence. Huey Long and his followers, an even more dangerous lot of ruffians, started a fascist movement that enlisted even a few of the more gullible of our intellectuals: a well-aimed gun luckily disposed of that. The moral burden of fighting fascism begins at home: but this fact does not remove the necessity of fighting fascism everywhere.

Democracy at its shabby third-best is still better than fascism at its proudest: the cruelties, the repressions, the injustices committed in the United States today, though far from negligible, are still nothing compared to the efficient assault that fascism has made on the very principles of civilization. In one case, the evils are accidental; in the case of fascism, they are essential: part of the very structure of the state itself. To equate Hague and Hitler, Girdler and Goering, is to fail to make the most elementary distinction: a distinction of numbers: it completely overlooks their

44

respective power and influence. Such a method would treat as equal a manure pile and a mountain because they had the same general shape and were both composed of "dirt." This, indeed, is the method that the fascists themselves use in their usual vilification of democracy. Those who specially esteem their own calm good sense because they are so ready to emphasize the obvious flaws and blemishes in democratic countries might at least ask themselves one question: Which cause do they further by promoting this kind of confusion whenever they discuss fascism? That of a better democracy? Or that of a stronger fascism?

## 6. THE CHALLENGE OF THE AMERICAN HERITAGE

We Americans live under the oldest written constitution in the world. We have a tradition of freedom, braced by the long experience of the frontier, with its free land and its sturdy opportunities for the self-reliant man. This tradition, though it has disappeared from our economic system temporarily, is still sanctified by our social practices: it includes almost every rank of American, no matter what his economic station, no matter what his political or religious opinions. It creeps out even in the casual behavior of the most convinced Tory: he may ferociously resent the demand of the working classes for more wages, but usually he takes it without a wince when the taxi-driver calls him Buddy.

Despite occasional waves of irrationality that existed even before the days of the Know-Nothings, the dislike of servility and authoritarianism is deeply engrained in the American character. Free speech, free choice, free government may be flouted by reaction-

46

ary local minorities; but they are still precious to the common run of Americans who work the farms and the factories of the country. This tradition is embodied in the protestantism, the rationalism, and the humanism that formed the original core of the American ideology: it was re-enforced by the level manliness of the frontier. It will always be a precious ingredient in the American character. When it vanishes, one of America's chief contributions to the world will vanish, too.

Every writer, every political leader who has left his impression upon the American mind, has upheld this tradition of freedom. It is in patrician Melville as much as in plebeian Whitman; it is in plantation Jefferson as much as in frontier Jackson; it is in platonic Bronson Alcott as much as in pragmatic John Dewey. Nurtured in this tradition are our greatest figures: witness the sweet austere humanity of an Emerson, the shrewd tender wisdom of a Lincoln. Witness, too, the implacable common sense of a Mark Twain or a Finley Peter Dunne. One common feature unites all these characters: a backbone that refuses to crumble before authority: a steady eye that refuses to blink before an upraised gun.

47

This tradition is opposed to any fixed and final status, in knowledge, in belief, in doctrine, in the human condition. One may call it the tradition of the universal frontier. Such a tradition is favorable to the co-operative endeavors of art and science and government; for it trusts the continuous applications of the experimental intelligence, and it rejects the abrupt finalities of dogma. The democratic synthesis must forever remain an open one, always subject to the correction of new experiences, new truths: always capable of amendment by a fresher experience, a deeper truth, a higher morality.

Opposed to a Hitler's paranoid assumptions of leadership, which implies the lowering of fascist subjects to the status of illiterate children, democracy takes refuge in Lincoln's profound dictum: No man is good enough to govern another. Hence, for the democrat, government is always a provisional act: not a mission but a temporary experiment. Its scope, its weight, its pressure must all be modified by circumstances. It is the weakness of dictatorships that they must not merely blot out opposition but maintain a constant pressure of coercion. It is the strength of democracy, not merely that it can utilize the opposition, but that it can alter its pressures: in a crisis it may even consent to an almost absolute rule, because the resumption of its original powers is never doubted.

Our constitutional government has at least partly succeeded by the pragmatic test. It has brought into a working communion vast millions of people, coming from diverse countries, bearing the most disparate national traditions: it has taught them to live in amity. What the United States is today, the world itself might become tomorrow if the menace of fascism and imperialism and class exploitation were lifted. Beneath all their national and regional and economic differences, Americans remember their common humanity: for "every man is as good as the next man and a damned sight better."

Whatever the muddy defects of the American scheme, we still preserve in grand outlines the traditions of a free people. Every American honors these traditions and knows that they give shape to his character: they are a source of his personal strength. Who fails to recognize this has already lost the most precious attribute of his citizenship. But the true American feels this in no jingo spirit, although the idea is infamously caricatured and betrayed by jingoes: he knows that what is best in his own democracy he shares with men of good will in all other countries. There is nothing that we want for ourselves that we do not want, ultimately, for the rest of the world. We are a choosing people, not a chosen people: we draw our full complement of strength from all the nations that have helped make us. In our very music we restore to honor the Negro we have so grievously mistreated.

Is this American heritage worth keeping: worth fighting for? I do not ask that question. This appeal is not addressed to the cynical and the indifferent: nor to those who do not believe in our American past, nor to those who do not believe in civilization: the latter, whether they openly profess it or not, are already in the fascist camp. I appeal only to those who, though they are deeply imbued with the American tradition, still shrink from undertaking the active task of every generation: that of re-examining our usable past, revaluing it, and re-translating it into fresh purposes and worthy deeds. The presence of fascism in the world has given us a special incentive to discover whatever is, by contrast, most excellent in our own heritage. And let us acknowledge no small debt to the fascists: they have rekindled our passion for democracy. By their wanton exhibitions of barbarism they have restored our respect for all the processes of civilization.

# 7. THE POTENCY OF THE PATHOLOGICAL

Probably the most serious mistake a civilized man can now make is to assume that the fundamental values of life have not been altered in the fascist countries. Traveling through Germany or Italy, the naïve observer sees lovers kissing, mothers nursing babies, honest peasants cleaving the soil with mattock or shovel: life looks "normal." The silent brutality of the concentration camp does not assail his ears: how could it? The fact that the entire country has become, quite literally, a concentration camp does not even occur to him: the visitor, unless denounced as a spy, is not forced to remain there. The fascist might say, in the pleading words of Shylock, Hath not a fascist hands, organs, dimensions, senses, affections, passions? The plea is just: no matter how gross the evils of fascism, we are still talking about the conduct of human beings. But the pound of flesh that the fascists have written into the bond likewise remains.

Large groups of people still somehow refuse to believe that nations which use the radio and the electric motor can, by a purely ideological transformation, become hostile to all those traditions that cement together the members of civil society. They try to account for the alteration that has taken place by themselves taking the main onus for the fascists' conduct, or at least by pinning it upon the stupidity or wrongdoing of the non-fascist nations. Was not Germany the victim of Versailles? Was not Italy humiliated by her virtual defeat and her incompetence? These people comfort themselves with the belief that fascism is a sort of divine retribution for the mistakes and injustices that were perpetrated at Versailles: in their sympathy for the mistreated German republic they extend their sheltering courtesy to the Nazis, although the Nazis fell heirs to a situation that had been steadily improving for the better, as concerns international justice, during the nine years before they were thrust into power.

This, by the way, is a matter that cannot be stressed too often. It brings into view another claim that it is equally important to rectify, that is, demolish: namely, the notion that the so-called moral recovery of Germany since Hitler came into power is an achievement of heroic dimensions, absolutely without parallel.

Those whose memory of Germany goes further back than yesterday's newspaper can remember a far more wonderful restoration: one that transformed Germany more swiftly and more beneficently than Hitler has done. This was the recovery that took place after the revaluation of the mark and the signing of the Locarno Treaty. Here Germany emerged from a hell so deep that by comparison the state of the country in 1933 was heaven: the rise took place swiftly, decisively. It was not merely that the renewal of the Republic's economic foundations, after the final humiliation of the French invasion of the Ruhr, restored life and order: it unleashed a host of creative activities: the result was not a mere comeback but a powerful thrust forward. Stricken and demoralized, Germany rose then as not even Republican France had risen after the defeat of the Franco-Prussian war.

Was the recovery that took place between 1924 and 1930 the result of the *Fuehrer Prinzip:* one-man dictatorship? Not in the least: it came about, rather, through the co-operative efforts of thousands of nameless participators and collaborators, as well as outstanding leaders. This democratic resurgence showed itself in the work of scientists, technicians, artists, in almost every sphere: in the great physical researches of an Einstein or a Schroedinger; in the art of a Barlach, whose sublime war memorial in Hamburg the Nazis shamefully removed; in the novels of Thomas Mann—the Magic Mountain appeared in 1925; in the constructive architectural experiments of a Mendelsohn, a Gropius, and a van der Rohe, in the townplanning of a Schumacher, a May, a Wagner.

These achievements were transforming the face of the land and the life of the German people, up to the moment in 1929 when the bottom dropped out of the world markets; their impetus, indeed, continued through 1932. But though they made Germany a leader of the world, these creative elements were compelled to struggle against deeply regressive forces in the German character. During the new economic crisis, the majority of Germans succumbed once more to their post-war sense of humiliation and malaise: instead of continuing on the upper road, they took the lower road. Turning from modern civilization, which they, more than any other people, had gone farthest toward defining and exploring and building, they relapsed into the cult of Wotan: the savage and the primeval. Momentarily halted in their creative act of construction, the Germans vengefully turned on their own handiwork and tore it down.

Enough, then, of the fascist myth that attributes to Hitler's singular influence a great material and moral recovery. By a miracle of will and imagination, Germany did in fact lift itself out of a hopeless moral, economic, and social morass: *but the time of this recovery was 1925, not 1933: it took place under the Republic, not under the Third Reich.* The fact that this early recovery was accomplished without repression, without martial display, without a faked unanimity, without the creation of an *Ersatz* religion, is the final commentary upon fascism's pretensions. For the new despots achieved nothing that rational men, in full possession of their minds and senses, did not achieve—with far more impressive gains—between 1924 and 1930. The economic basis of this renewal was unsound: neither the loans nor the reparations could be kept up. But the psychological triumph of reasonable men—and it is this very matter of morale that is in question—is indisputable.

The attempt to extenuate the fascists by appealing to history unfortunately does not go far enough: those who hold these views stop short in their history at the date of the first World War. If fascism were the result of the Treaty of Versailles, it would be difficult to explain the emergence of a typical fascist state, mollified by a show of French urbanity, through the bloodless coup d'état of Napoleon III in France. The revolution of 1848 formed a pretext for this early fascism; but, like the bad conditions in Italy in 1922, like the "impossible" situation of Germany in 1933, the crisis was actually over and the conditions well improved before the fascists achieved their concentration of power. It is men who create fascism: to place the burden of the effort and the moral responsibility upon "conditions" is to belittle the role of even the lowest human intelligence. Many liberals, many communists, holding that the fascists were impotent to create fascism, automatically surrender to it: because, on their own account, given the same economic conditions, men are equally impotent to create an alternative to fascism.

Such specious social interpretations confuse causes with circumstances. They overweight the effect of external situations and they seriously underrate the part played by ideas, projects, fantasies, and the concentrated will of men. No one doubts that the misery and demoralization that followed the iniquitous Treaty of Versailles provided a soil in which fascism could more easily grow: but if the disease were solely a product of the conditions, it should have broken out in Germany long before it did in Italy.

The active causes of fascism were archaic views of political life and destiny that took hold of men's minds and molded their projects: none of these beliefs and sentiments was produced by either the world war or its baneful economic aftermath: none of them will disappear merely by permitting the fascist states to seize by force what was denied to them under the guise of justice. The failure to reckon with what the French sociologist, Fouillée, called *idées-forces* is one of the most pathetic results of an uncritical acceptance of the economic interpretation of history. In its large outlines, the economic interpretation clarifies the motives of men: unfortunately it cannot explain why men will work more cheerfully for a starvation wage, under the impression that they are serving their fatherland, than they did for a living wage, when they thought only of keeping their families alive. No one can doubt that, at least temporarily, this has happened in Germany. And it is precisely what is irrational in this situation, what cannot be explained in terms of pecuniary gain or rational self-interest, that constitutes the strength of fascism: indeed its one partial element of validity.

The attempt to rationalize fascism on purely economic grounds leads to another kind of misinterpretation. The notion that fascism is merely the aggressive expression of the "have-not" nations' desire for economic justice has been taken up uncritically by various presumably enlightened groups in other countries, as if the very foundations of this argument were not false and fascist to the core. The economic way in which to redress the lack of certain materials and resources in a given country is by the normal processes of foreign trade: no country is big enough to be self-contained or self-sufficient until it has swallowed the whole planet. It is only in a state of war that these lacks and inequalities are a critical obstacle to a nation's life. Fascism opposes every effort to restrict population and then holds the increase of population as a just excuse for seizing some neighbor's land. So fascism attempts to build up an autarchic economic system in order to be victorious in war; and then threatens war in order to make possible this autarchy. These are irrational solutions for conditions that offer many rational alternatives. Fascism prefers military seizure to trade, blackmail to bargains. This is an aberration, not an excuse.

If the fascist nations sought justice and peace, they would use their influence against all forms of imperialist monopoly and in favor of equal opportunities for all groups throughout the planet. Such demands however imply a belief in all the processes that fascism as a political doctrine denies: fact-finding, truth-seeking, co-operation and concert, honest, even-handed administration, respect for law, reciprocity and good will. But none of these aims fits in with the fascist complex—arms: booty: sadistic exploit. In order to maintain their doctrines and their party bureaucracy intact, the fascists must, in the nature of things, increase the area of their conquests and pyramid their claims. The lust for power is insatiable: in that sense, the fascist states will always be have-nots. Japan, having seized Manchuria for "protection," now purposes to swallow China: if she succeeds, she will still be "insecure" till Siberia and Indo-China follow.

It is this irrational element in fascism that has confounded those who have tried to deal with it by more affable methods. Democracy is a product, in part, of the rationalist imagination. Its roots are in the give-and-take of trade, in the desire to substitute

60

contract for the feudal condition of status: its method consists in counting hands instead of exchanging blows. Modern democracy grew up with the newspaper, with systematic science, with parliamentary forms of government in all convocations of people. It was a protest against arbitrary power and secretive methods, against Star chambers, *lettres de cachet,* secret inquisitions, closed courts, against irresponsible power in every form. Democracy exists by a continual appeal to reasonable men to act reasonably, in the light of common knowledge: to displace their own prejudices and preferences when the facts—or the opinion of the majority—confound them.

Democracy's typical weakness grows out of this utilitarian ideology: except in the form of nationalist patriotism democratic governments have underrated the power of the irrational for both good and bad. Art, ritual, ceremony, for example, are either reduced to perfunctory performances or are degraded into something private and comic, like a parade of Odd Fellows or Mystic Shriners. The deeper motives of men, those that produce art and religion, on one hand, or insanity and fascism on the other, are more or less excluded from the public routines of democracy. So it is easier for the advocate of democracy to recognize

61

quantitative, economic differences than qualitative differences: differences of degree rather than of kind. On this supposition, fascism differs from democracy only in degree: it is a little more arbitrary, a little more tyrannous, a little more boss-ridden, a little more nationalistic, a little more belligerent than our own. That fascism is radically different in *kind* is far more difficult for the ordinary citizen to realize. And yet this last is precisely the truth.

Hence the folly of recent attempts to bring fascist states back into the older channels of civilized intercourse. The people who have proposed these methods are too thinly rational to understand the nature of irrationality: perhaps they are too blandly good even to recognize the existence of evil. Such minds, as Reinhold Niebuhr has well put it, are actually incredulous as to the existence of radical evil: they pride themselves on living in a world of moral twilight, in which all cats are gray: the moral equivalent of the liberal's curious notion that the truth must always lie "somewhere between."

This liberal attitude fails to recognize that just as the whiteness of the saint is increased by his human capacities for sin, so the blackness of the fascists is actually increased by the fact that, being men, they

62

have some residual capacity for exercising virtue or speaking truth. We cannot say: Forgive them for they know not what they do. On the contrary, when they torture the defenseless and exile the intelligent, we *cannot forgive them precisely* because *they know what they do*.

In short: we are not merely faced with evil conditions: we are faced with the doctrines and the works of evil men. One of the reasons that liberalism has been so incapable of working energetically for good ends is that it is incapable of resisting evil: in its priggish fear of committing an unfair moral judgment it habitually places itself on the side of the successful. This moral queasiness has been one of liberalism's effective contributions to fascism's victories. Out of the spinelessness of "liberalism" the backbone of fascism has been created.

# 8.  THE CONFUSION WITH IMPERIALISM

Another source of intellectual confusion in dealing
with fascism is the habit of treating the methods and
ideology of the fascists as if they were those of nine-
teenth-century imperialism. In the abstract, they have
many points in common; but the differences are quite
as significant as the points upon which they tally.
And the most important difference is the fact that
under imperialism courageous minorities, often large
ones, existed in every country: even Russia. These
minorities not merely actively fought against the tendency to seize and exploit distant lands: they freely
opposed the dirty brutalities that accompanied this
process. Such critical voices were heard all over the
world: not least in their own communities.

As a result, until the fascists deliberately created
more fulsome methods of political violence, imperialism had become, by the end of the nineteenth century,
apologetic, shamefaced, abashed: in the very hypocrisy by which their naked economic aims were cloaked,
the imperial powers made their first dim acknowledg-

ment of political morals. So the way was opened to a different state, of reciprocity and free government: this took place in Cuba and the Philippines after the American conquest there: it took place in South Africa after the British had completed their disreputable conquest of the Boers. So, too, Belgium could not insulate itself, in the case of the Congo atrocities, against the moral indignation of the rest of the world. Though imperialism was itself a barbarous phenomenon—accompanied, like Nazism, with similar spurious doctrines of racial supremacy—the governments that promoted it were subject to the play of the humaner forces in our civilization.

For the last generation there was, in international affairs, a steady gain for moral decency. Even the Treaty of Versailles, though it lacked justice and magnanimity, was coupled with at least the lip recognition of a more rational political order, embodied in the League of Nations. The people who whined most loudly over its results were Germans like the neurotic Wotan worshiper, Ludendorff: a hero who fled from the field of his defeat with the courage of a mangy rabbit. Most intelligent Germans knew then, and still know, that the treaty the German government

65

had in store for the Allies, had they been victorious, was far more ferocious in its injustices.

Here again the Nazis have received a good deal of misplaced sympathy from those with long ears and short memories. The most grievous complaint of the Germans, apart from the geographical fantasy called the Polish corridor, was in the matter of the amount of reparations imposed: but it is well to remember that the Germans borrowed twice as much money as they repaid: in the end, the Allies, and particularly their American backers, lost by this imposition. Indefensible as any imperialism now is, the League of Nations, with all its shortcomings, offered a means whereby the Lilliputian nations of the world were, until 1930, gradually getting the imperialist Gullivers to accept a network of restrictions that would have made further military conquests impossible. Instead of lending their strength to this movement, Japan, Germany, and Italy threw their weight on the other side: they broke up the one agent that was capable, in time, of breaking down the imperialist monopolies.

In contrast to the wormy triumphs of imperialism, fascism presents an unbroken front: it allows no loopholes for humanitarian attack. And here precisely is the overwhelming moral and political distinction between a democratic government and a fascist regime: *the evil forces that exist in a democracy are exposed to criticism and open to correction: those in a fascist state are sealed against even the majority's opinion.* Through control of the written and spoken word, fascism has insulated itself from the challenge of truth: it is immune to an appeal to a higher moral standard. Unlike democratic governments, fascist states have no place for moral correctives within their system: their barbarism is unchallengeable from within: what the "leader" does is right—on his say-so. When the aviator son of Mussolini writes with gusto of his personal massacre of Abyssinian villagers, only the private retching of the stomach is permitted to those many generous, humane Italians whose reflexes are not yet completely conditioned to barbarism.

Fascism is by definition a one-way system. Through its omnipotent censorship it withholds from its subjects any possibility of comparison with the standards and practices of the civilized world. While it seeks to spread its doctrines everywhere, it refuses to admit within its frontier, even for bare discussion, any doctrine that would challenge its delusions and claims.

Nobody knows what the German people or the Italian people now think upon any subject whatever.

All one knows is what they have been permitted to think. What fragment of their real thoughts is thus expressed there is no way of gauging: in the elections they may only vote yes: the electoral mountain humorlessly labors to bring forth a dead mouse. Even between friends, the people in fascist countries dare not trust themselves to speak freely: too many honest men have already been betrayed by erstwhile friends and comrades. And indeed, what an Italian or a German may now think in his private capacities has ceased to count. Within a generation all the values that the best men and women have embodied in the past will have been systematically extirpated in the school and the military camp. Result: a generation of intellectual eunuchs and ethical morons.

Whereas in every other civilized country during the last generation the power state has become discredited, as an atavistic survival, in fascist countries the power state has reached heights of despotism, depths of submission and degradation, that a Genghis Khan or a Peter the Great might well have envied. And yet the victory is incomplete. One thing we know of what still lies in the hearts of the Italian and the German people. Though they have been drilled, regimented, indoctrinated, suppressed, though they have been taught to glory in the uglier qualities of war, they are at bottom still human beings. When what they believed was the beginning of another World War was averted at Munich, there came, from the depths of their regimented breasts, a happy sob of release: they cheered the peace as they had never cheered the wars that their dictators had boasted and threatened.

That salutation may be ominous to the dictatorships. Eventually, one may hope, this human sound will be translated into a workable scheme of world peace based upon a renunciation of the myths of "political sovereignty" and "race" and national isolation. But immediately this love of peace on the part of fascist subjects may presage just the opposite action on the part of their uneasy rulers: a more violent assault upon the very existence of democracy.

# 9. HUMANITY'S THREAT TO FASCISM

Fascism, indeed, faces a serious threat from within. Men may not be born free, but they are born potentially human. Fascism is forever threatened by the continued humanness of humanity. Even a Mussolini, a Goebbels, or a Hitler is not a natural monstrosity: he is partly the result of accident, mischance, perverse experience, shocks and traumas, deliberate culture, economic pressures: in the beginning each had, one must assume, the potentialities of becoming civilized as well as the potentiality of reverting to barbarism. What is the source of Hitler's racialism but the feelings of inferiority that overcame a loutish country boy when first he mingled with the strange faces and heard the polyglot tongues on the streets of Vienna, once one of the most sophisticated of world cities? He himself points to this beginning of his compensatory fantasies.

Fascism is menaced by the tendency of normal men and women to temper their newly acquired barbarism by ancient sentiments of pity and generosity, born of

the original love of mammals for the helpless suck-
ling: most men have a need to succor as well as a
need for aggression. So long has our social heritage
been in existence, so completely has man become de-
pendent upon it for the very breath of his life, that it
has become second nature to him: its claims appear
to his conscious self, or his super-ego, as often superior to that of his "first nature," the raw, untutored
self to which he may revert. Fascism is threatened by
a deep human tendency to displace a corrupt system
of fantasies by common sense, by respect for truth,
by practical experiment, by the co-operative criticism
of one's fellows. Finally, fascism is insidiously undermined by the irreverent sense of humor through
which lowly humanity revenges itself upon the pretensions of the great and the powerful: how often
must the proper answer to one of Mussolini's or
Hitler's tirades have been uttered in some German or
Italian equivalent of "Aw, nuts!" Ignazio Silone, in
his superb Fontamara stories, has well pictured these
latent tendencies.

So far these fine human impulses have been innocu-
ous: fascism knows how to deal with them. When
propaganda and misinformation are not sufficient, the
concentration camp finishes the job. At the threat of

some more general disintegration or slackness, the clangor of war-alarms is used to stiffen the fascist nation once more into a state of cataleptic rigidity. Nevertheless, fascism must remain on the alert against the normal manifestations of humanity. Above all, it must exclude all knowledge of the possibility of an alternative method of life. Internally it erects a wall around the country: it imposes restrictions upon the movements of both goods and men: it drowns out foreign radio programs or arrests those who listen to them: it shuts out newspapers, magazines, books— though here the barrier of language is, for the majority, a sufficient defense. Fascism even limits the internal movements of its subjects about the country: it seals their mouths: it stops up their ears: it halts those processes of communication and mutual intercourse which are the very life-blood of culture.

Still the fascist state cannot feel secure: even the tightest ship lets water into its hold. Occasionally a dangerous thought will seep in through the well-caulked seams of fascist censorship.

To ensure fascism against the challenge of a different ideology fascism must therefore wage a pitiless campaign against non-fascist states. It must disorganize the political life of democratic countries; it

72

must promote that species of pacifism which will make them unable to resist fascism; it must encourage those groups that seek to imitate fascism. It is not merely by verbal thunderbolts that Mussolini or Hitler seek to work against democracy: they subsidize agents to accomplish their will. During the last year in America we have had a good chance to observe the magnitude of these activities. Fascism takes advantage of the very opportunities for free discussion and free action which democracy offers in order to undermine the principle of democracy.

The reason for this fascist attack is plain. In the long run fascism cannot compete with democracy nor can it afford to risk its challenge. The love of freedom did not arise yesterday; it will not die tomorrow. If for no other reason than its own security, fascism cannot rest content with its immediate conquests: it must attack democracy wherever it has the faintest chance of achieving victory. If that purpose was only passively expressed, in contemptuous phrases of negation, when Mussolini wrote his article on the fascist state for the Italian encyclopedia, its existence as an active and determining policy has become apparent during the last five years. The Munich agreement only intensified the opportunity and guaranteed greater success to it. Czechoslovakia has been wiped out; France is next on the program.

This fascist need for expansion, to ensure its own existence, has changed the very nature of the problems that confront the American people on the international stage. It is not a need for markets or for economic advantage that alone prompts this fascist move: the political aim is more important than the economic one. Indeed, with respect to the motives of fascist states, one may say that politics is the driving force, economics the rationalization. Whereas, under a capitalist oligarchy, it is always safe to interpret political moves in terms of economic interest, in relation to fascism one must treat economics as an expression of a far more subjective politics. The failure to understand this on the part of Marxian theorists has been one of the reasons for their ludicrous errors in interpreting or meeting this new force: an error that helped give Germany to Hitler.

In short: there is now no conceivable limit to fascist aggression until the world is made over in the fascist image. For the only security of fascism against the ever-rising, ever-recurrent forces of civilization is to reduce mankind as a whole to its own state of barbarism. In the face of this fact a policy of wishful

74

waiting on the part of democracies is a policy of submission. To arrive at a peaceful adjustment of this kind of conflict is impossible: the best one can hope for is the stalemate of armed hostility, continued in existence until the weaker side disintegrates. *Here the advantages are with democracy. If it holds its own, it will achieve the psychological equivalent of a gory fascist conquest.*

Humane men are naturally reluctant to admit that such an extreme condition has come about. They are loath to believe in the active propagation of barbarism in countries once as great as Germany and Italy: as loath as they would be to admit that a once-valued colleague was suffering from systematic morbid delusions and had to be put under restraint in an asylum. To their credit, they have given fascism the benefit of the doubt. In 1928 it was still possible to treat fascism lightly: Mussolini's operatic grimaces were rather a caricature of power than a display of it. In 1933 it was still possible to disregard the brutal menace of Nazism: perhaps six months in office, if it did not give back parliamentary democracy to the German people, would at least give them back intellectual freedom, cultural dignity, self-respect. But by the time Mussolini invaded Abyssinia the pathological nature of fascism had become increasingly plain in both countries: and the fact that *its cruelties have increased with its successes* has demonstrated how ill-founded the policy of appeasement has been.

We have given fascism the benefit of the doubt: it is now time to give democracy the benefit of our convictions. For the calamity of the Munich peace should at last have opened the eyes of even the most dogmatic pacifist, even the most timorous isolationist. What was remarkable in that arrangement was not the hysterical methods of the Nazis nor their contemptuous denial of the most elementary principles of either justice or decency: what was remarkable was the cordial acquiescence of Chamberlain and Daladier. One does not know which was more offensive to human dignity: the doggish fear in their eyes or the propitiating wag of their tails. The fact that they had carried the succulent morsel to Hitler in their mouths —the Berchtesgaden treachery—fortunately did not prevent them from getting an extra vicious kick in the rump as they turned away. That was perhaps the one touch of justice that attended this well-planned betrayal of their own democracies. They had surrendered democracy everywhere to save their empires: result, they lost their effective defense of both.

# 10. DEMORALIZATION
## OF THE "REALISTS"


While fascism's attacks against democracy were purely domestic, the world was justified, perhaps, in leaving the fascist nations to stew in their own juice. This does not excuse the benevolence of England and France toward the actual breaking of international treaties: nor does it expiate their self-deception—to put it most generously—about the significance of the Nazis' rearmament, or, even earlier, the Japanese conquest of Manchuria. Nor does it excuse the supineness and slackness of labor groups in all countries in meeting the situation—one cannot forget that Blum's Popular Front government accepted the outrageous "non-intervention" agreement, which crippled the Republican government of Spain.

But the series of successes that the fascist countries have achieved have turned an ideological portent into a practical menace to every other state in which the processes of a free political life are kept up. Already the losses are vast: already the situation is desperate:

not because of the actual strength of the fascist states, which only a fool would accept at their own overblown estimate, but because of the intellectual and moral weaknesses disclosed in our democratic leadership up to the moment of writing. Even the American government cannot escape a share of the blame: for in the main, during the last few years, we have followed the leadership of the pro-Hitler English Tories, and to the extent that we have done so our policy has lacked foresight, common honesty, or even intelligent self-interest.

The policy which the British government has followed reached its logical culmination in the surrender at Munich. Under the guise of realistically meeting a difficult situation, the British and French governments agreed to a fantastic bargain. In 1935 there were two fascist states of importance in Europe. They had as allies, or at least as partial dependents, Austria, Hungary, and Poland. To the west of this bloc there lay a solid wall of democratic nations whose neutrality, in case of war, was assured: whose active participation upon the side of democracy could in the long run have been counted on, against any threat the fascist governments might offer. At the "peace" of Munich, England and France not merely gave up the possibility of military aid from the East, from a well-armed Czechoslovakia and a potentially strong Soviet Russia: but, by the very method in which they permitted Hitler to rape Czechoslovakia, they included in the unwritten terms of surrender the following:

| | |
|---|---:|
| Spain ............. | 28,719,177 |
| Holland ............ | 8,061,571 |
| Belgium ............ | 8,213,449 |
| Denmark ........... | 3,684,000 |
| Sweden ............ | 6,211,566 |
| Norway ............ | 2,817,124 |
| Finland ............ | 3,667,067 |
| Switzerland ......... | 4,143,500 |

Roughly speaking, in other words, over sixty-five million people, exclusive of the Czechs, were put in jeopardy; or rather, turned over to fascism on whatever terms the latter may in future impose. Unless there is an immediate rightabout face in British policy, these people must now face acquiescence in Germany's domination and co-operation with her policies, or extinction: the threat that sufficed in effecting the dismemberment of Czechoslovakia, a country immensely superior in military strength to any in the

79

above list, even Spain, will apply equally to any one of these. In a military sense, this was not England's defeat: it was her utter rout and extinction. So much for the astuteness of England's practical statesman.

In reckoning the loss I have omitted numerically the two chief items: England and France. Only by a prodigy of popular resolution and skillful leadership can either of these nations retain their independent existence as democracies. They are in a position where they must depend upon the good-will of Nazi Germany to forestall a war which they may now have to fight against fearful odds: at least during the first six months. These countries are no longer powers: in the literal feudal sense they are vassals: the relationship was well symbolized by Mr. Chamberlain's humble visit to Berchtesgaden. Already the signs of their vassalage have appeared. In neither England nor France may newspapers print freely facts or opinions about their German overlord: government censorship here is increasingly rigid because of the menace to "peace." In the interests of "peace"—that is, of fascist domination—the very basis of political democracy has been removed.

Under pressure of war-threats Germany can now even compel a change in government. The German press and its leading officials have already visited their wrath upon statesmen like Winston Churchill, who have had the foresight and the keen intelligence to realize what fascism means. Who doubts that this threat will be exercised, if present methods continue, to ensure the transformation of France into a compliant fascist state? England may retain a position of formal independence a little longer: but only because most of the governing classes in England—with such honorable exceptions as an Alfred Duff Cooper or a Winston Churchill—are already willing servants of the Nazis: indeed it was by their sleek connivance that the democracies of Europe were turned over to Hitler.

So far I have been judging the fatal Munich appeasement in terms of *Realpolitik:* terms upon which it appears that England and France have suffered defeat and humiliation almost as completely as Czechoslovakia. One may say, indeed, in no figurative sense, that the first World War ended finally at Munich with the complete capitulation of the Allies: even the United States suffered in that final humiliation through Mr. Roosevelt's ill-advised plea to Hitler: a stroke which helped Chamberlain to make the final gesture of "surrender." But what was more important

81

than *what* happened at Munich was *how* it happened. The moral disintegration that produced the betrayal of Berchtesgaden and the complaisant submission of Munich was more dreadful than any mere political defeat. That it was followed by hollow attempts at self-congratulation and even Pecksniffian votes of thanks to the injured nation only accentuates the character of the act: Dickens should have been on hand to comment on the entire occasion. At least he prepared us for it.

Law and justice and common humanity were completely flouted because Hitler seemed ready to take the suicidal risk of war. The dangers were exaggerated by the politicians of England and France—and Hitler's prospects of an imminent and early defeat were deliberately withheld from view—in order to make easy the already contemplated surrender. How well the treachery had been planned is familiar to everyone who can still remember back to a little while before the Berchtesgaden meeting: the London *Times*, "indiscreetly," had suggested to the Sudetens that they secede.

In short, the Treaty of Versailles, achieved at the end of a bitter and rancorous war, was a great humanitarian document compared with the pact of

Munich: likewise a triumph of political sagacity. Vile as the Munich terms were, Hitler made further revisions for the worse within a few days. Not a finger was lifted even in protest. In their cowardly flight from the bare forms of justice, democracy's statesmen left all their moral baggage behind.

In all these matters, the patent enemy was not the fascists: Mussolini indeed had not even mobilized. The most treacherous actions, the slimiest betrayals came from the statesmen who were, people generously thought, representing the cause of democracy: jackals to the snarling Nazi lion. The depth of their moral debasement gives the measure of democracy's danger today. The descent to the fascist level of barbarism has been swift. The willingness of a Chamberlain or a Daladier to deal with Hitler on his own terms gives a picture of their lack of either moral courage or moral conviction. Men who are so completely demoralized are capable of anything. They have proved that.

## 11. WHERE THE MUNICH SURRENDER LEAVES US

The first major operation in fascism's assault against democracy was for all practical purposes completed at Munich. Europe is now in the hands of the barbarians: if they remain in power so much as another decade they will extinguish almost every evidence of political freedom and free intelligence, not merely in their own countries, but in those of their vassals. Unless a benevolent catastrophe upsets the fascist plans, Europe is lost.

There is only one major country left that can, for a few more years, thanks to its geographic position, resist the active aggressions of the fascist states: that is the United States. It is here, and here alone, that active resistance can be made: we are the core of any counter-attack on behalf of democracy. Against the United States, therefore, the hatred of the fascists is already turned, with tripled fury, violence, and vindictiveness. They have quenched in our generation the very hope of resistance in Europe. But so long as a single liberty can be preserved against the totalitarian state, so long as a single democracy remains intact, fascism's domestic hold must remain a little precarious.

The United States will have to bear the brunt of fascism's blows: their propaganda, today; their active armaments, perhaps, ten years hence. We must therefore be prepared to accept the challenge of democratic leadership. Whether we like it or not, fascism has accorded us this honor.

Before September, 1938, our task was formidable enough; by now it has taken on gigantic proportions. We have not merely lost the seventy-five million democratic allies that Chamberlain gave away at Munich: we have probably also lost the effective help of England and France. When in the spring of 1938 I proposed that America must take an active part in fighting fascism, Major Fielding Eliot optimistically countered my plea by pointing to the fact that the military superiority of England and France, with their allies, made any special efforts of our own unnecessary. But in "The Ramparts We Watch," published the fall of the same year, he could no longer count upon such protection. Though my prophecy did not convert him, the events which justified the prophecy apparently did so.

Until a decisive change in government takes place in England and France, a change which places in power leaders actively committed to the defense of democracy, we must regard the policies of England and France with extreme skepticism, not to say hostility. To co-operate with a Chamberlain is to invite upon our own heads a betrayal similar to that which Czechoslovakia encountered. In a desperate attempt to save the poor scattered remnants of a weakened empire, the Pro-Hitler Tories in England might endeavor to assume the role of pacificator in our already strained relations with the German government.

In such a guise England might place her fleet between that of Germany and our own for the ostensible purpose of "protecting" her American friend: then, if Hitler threatened to unloose his war planes over England—in propagandist warfare only fascists are capable of invading the enemy with airplanes—England might turn her guns westward in order to preserve peace. This would be a refinement of the Chamberlain-Runciman formula. It would be all the easier in the case of the United States, not merely because the Tory oligarchy is traditionally hostile to

American democracy, but because the British may have a twinge of guilty conscience about the old war-debt. Impossible? Fantastic? Nonsense: the tactic employed with relation to Czechoslovakia was equally fantastic and impossible until it finally took place.

Non-co-operation with the exploiting classes in England and France in their policy of appeasing fascism is the first principle of sound American statesmanship today. And the second is equally plain: until they have oriented their foreign policies so as to accord with our own, we should withhold the arms and munitions and planes that are now being manufactured in this country for shipment there. As independent democratic powers, they had some claim to assistance in this department, as long as our own needs were not endangered: but as fascist vassals they are already potential enemies. We must first assure ourselves on this simple matter: against whom will the guns be used? No promises that a Chamberlain or a Daladier may make can reassure us. Until men of honor are in office, backed by militant democratic majorities, by the workers above all, the solemnest vows that the governments of France or England must make must be put in the same class as those of a Hitler or a Mussolini: discounted one hundred per cent.

Fascism's anti-democratic thrust is now a practical necessity for its policy of conquest. To our American democracy fascism leaves only one alternative: actively resist it or submit to it. That issue is not of our choosing. We cannot avoid it merely by wishing for peace, or by refraining, on our part, from any acts of alienation or hostility. It is not what we do that may eventually cause war: it is what we are. The question that fascism puts to democracy is not *whether* we shall fight but *how and when* we shall fight. Shall we wait to fight fascism, as the troubled nations of Europe have waited, till fascism is strong enough to take us on in an actual war, having fully absorbed and co-ordinated its European conquests; or shall we fight fascism at our own time, on our own chosen battle-ground, on our own terms? The latter need not bring active military combat. Indeed, it is probably the only way by which our democracy can avoid the final clash.

To those who fancy that there is any other issue from this dilemma I would say, as one would shout to a sleeping man in the midst of a fire: Wake up! if you stay a moment longer with your dreams the flames will consume you! For such lovers of peace, for such advocates of planless optimism and muddled retreat, I would earnestly urge: Consider the fate of the hopeful democrats who have been killed or maimed in fascist concentration camps. Consider the probable fate of Spain: the fate of Czechoslovakia yesterday or the fate of France tomorrow. Democratic Europe can no longer protect you against fascism: the democracies have been betrayed by their ruling classes. The latter prefer to be the subservient clients of fascism rather than to share their power and privileges with their own countrymen.

Every civilized person desires peace. This argument indeed is addressed only to those who believe in peace and know that most of the things men of good will hold dear can be achieved only in a state of peace: we are opposed to "those hirelings in the court, the camp, and the university who would forever depress mental and prolong corporeal war." Those who believe that war is a permanent attribute of human life, like eating, rather than an obsolete cultural form, like cannibalism, need read no further: this book is not for them.

But peace is neither a state of political Nirvana nor a moral vacuum: no state of peace is tolerable in which the savage and the debased have the upper hand over the rest of humanity: on the contrary, the real problem of peace is to weld force to humane pur-

89

poses and to use it for humane ends. But there are higher aims, all decent men agree, than merely preserving human life or fending off death: peace in that purely negative sense is indeed worthy of the soldier's ancient contempt. And we have at last discovered that there is something worse than war: namely, the state of intellectual servitude and moral debasement and cowed political submission that exists under the "peace" of fascism.

Fortunately, there are still plenty of people all over the world who will not be bullied, by threats of war and death, into accepting a mode of life that is more repulsive than war and death. Everyone must die: it is better to die for a good reason than to continue to live for a bad one. Millions of such sound, liberty-loving people live in America today. They probably form the great majority, though generally a silent one: they know that in times of disaster, in a wreck, a tornado, an earthquake, the common needs must be uppermost. At those moments one must shun one's normal comforts and prudences and be prepared to face the worst. Those Americans who would cling at all costs to their false sense of security in the midst of the present world catastrophe fancy that civilization can be saved cheaply. Refusing to face the actual

90

world or to understand its menacing realities, they think of only one thing: their immediate safety. They are like a person who crowds close to a wall for protection when the earth itself starts to heave.

For those of us who still prize our democracy, there is no safety left in the world that does not demand, as its price, our whole-hearted struggle: our willingness to sacrifice everything, even our own lives, in order to avert a greater catastrophe for civilization. The policy of retreat, delay, hopeful inaction, postponement, only piles up our difficulties: *men must act.* We must meet barbarism with a force, with a plan, with a willingness to make sacrifices that are superior to its own savage vehemence. It is better for the United States government to overestimate the extent of our military needs than for men of good will to underestimate the necessity of having to fight.

## 12. NEED FOR A POSITIVE
## AMERICAN POLICY

One thing should now be plain after two swift years of demonstration: we must not cajole ourselves into believing that "fascism cannot for long seriously menace the peace of the world." Neither must we rely hopefully upon the presumed bankruptcy of the fascist nations as a deterrent to their plans. Bankruptcy is a handicap under old-fashioned capitalist finance which depended upon the free operation of the market both nationally and internationally: under a closed economy it need occasion no difficulty as long as public morale can be kept up and the protests of the creditor classes silenced by a course in patriotism in the concentration camp.

Besides, as long as the food supply can be extended by barter or tribute, there is little to keep the base of the totalitarian state from becoming more stable. As their successes increase the audacity of the Nazis, we shall doubtless see tribute take a more important place in meeting their collective needs. I leave this last sentence as it was written in October, 1938. Within a fortnight the German government had actually begun the process by imposing its first large-scale levy upon its Jewish population: this is but a foretaste of what the next few years will show. In the fascists' spartan regime even the capitalists have learned to convert part of their expectations of golden profits into the warrior's iron.

Any realistic survey of the political world must assume until events prove otherwise that the fascists will continue to widen the circle of their triumphs and consolidate their power. Having almost reduced England and France to the rank of second-rate powers, having increased their own strength and self-confidence, one cannot predict any limit to their rule: perhaps their worst enemy is their overweening pride: the tragic Greek sin of *hybris*. The fascist states may all break up overnight: they may last indefinitely. Napoleon in 1811 held sway over as large a part of Europe as the fascists do today. In four short years his vast pretensions had vanished like a pricked toy-balloon, with one last faint pop.

Since the pathology of Napoleon's delusions of grandeur was mild in comparison with that of Mussolini and Hitler—and was based in fact on a far abler

mind and a much solider foundation of achievements
—it is not impossible that one or both of these rulers
will lead a fatal march into Russia. It matters little
whether the Russia be a real or a figurative one: such
a weakening may prove the turning point of their regime. It is too early to say yet whether the Nazis'
moron-like physical attack on the Jews, at a moment
when they had only to use a little Chamberlain-like
finesse to accomplish their vilest purposes, was such
a turning point: that depends upon how long the universal revulsion against this barbarity remains in
existence.

Certainly, both the Nazis and the fascists, during
the months that have followed their too-easy victory at
Munich, have shown a jitteriness that bears no relation to their apparent success. The policy of frightfulness invoked against the Jews in Germany argues
a critical inner weakness—only to a fascist could
it look like strength. It may be that the fascist struc-
tures are even more rotten than we have dared believe: but if this is so, it surely calls for a stiffer
opposition on the part of democracy, so that these op-
pressive states may topple more speedily. The walls
seem shaken; even without Joshua's horn they may
tumble down; but that is no excuse for not blowing

it. Millions of good Germans and Italians pray for this deliverance. But no sane policy can be based on miracles and accidents. Until fascism is actually flying in retreat no one is entitled now to look forward to anything but a continued expansion of its power: this means the enlargement of Germany's and Italy's influence in the whole international field, and it means a popularization of their methods, their doctrines, their ideology. Their "successes" will be flattered by more widespread imitation.

To regard Italy and Germany as oldtime national states is to misunderstand the present change. These fascist countries are no longer simply political states: they are states of mind. To enter into co-operation with "Italy" is to ally oneself with the fascist creed, not with the Italian people. As a propulsive system of beliefs, fascism aims at world dominion.

This indicates that the United States, no less than Great Britain and France and Czechoslovakia, will be drawn into the fascist orbit unless we adopt a policy specifically designed to save our integrity as a democratic nation. That policy should have a single aim: making the United States impregnable against fascism. We must face the enemy on both the domestic and the foreign fronts.

## 13. AN AMERICAN LINE OF ACTION

What, then, should be the outlines of an intelligent, realistic American policy, boldly carved in the traditions of our own country? The measures that I brought forward for discussion had not, in May, 1938, yet gained any large public hearing. Before the pact of Munich they seemed, even to many who were sympathetic to the general idea, far too drastic to be considered seriously. But already events have begun to catch up with these proposals. And by now, fortunately, the alternatives that were seriously canvassed before the Munich pact are hopelessly outmoded.

Up to Munich, by a curious paralysis of the imagination, only two approaches had been made in the United States toward securing peace. One was isolationism, the other was interventionism, or collective security. Actually, we voted for isolationism in the naïve and futile Neutrality Acts: by our policy of non-action in China we intervened on behalf of the Japanese, and by our readiness to place an embargo against the Republican government of Spain, we broke

96

a solemn treaty with the Spanish people and capped it by intervening, in the company of Chamberlain, on behalf of a fascist victory in the Spanish peninsula. Under the guise of neutrality we have given positive aid to the Rome-Berlin axis: hating war, we have promoted it: hating tyranny, we have helped it.

In short, we have had a maximum of intervention with a minimum of either isolation or collective security. But it would be whipping a dead horse to go fully into the defects of both these abstract policies; if I do so at all, it is because there are still people left in the United States who are trying to ride dead horses.

The policy of collective security was based upon the notion of renouncing war, by standing firmly together on behalf of treaties, laws, promises of arbitration, and by taking active measures to meet the aggression of any outside power. This policy was ditched in 1931 when Great Britain refused to co-operate with the United States in resisting Japan's unprovoked invasion of Manchuria: thank Sir John Simon. It collapsed again in 1935 through France's failure to aid England to clamp down on Mussolini's adventure: thank Laval. It collapsed once more when, in the face of international law and abundant precedent, the hypocritical policy of non-intervention was maintained in Spain despite Italy's and Germany's openly hostile acts: thank Eden, Blum, and their colleagues: even our own State Department.

Behind all these failures was the fact that the League of Nations had originally been used as an instrument to prevent rectification of grievances, instead of to facilitate the administration of justice and the arbitrament of conflicts. Though the League had come to perform important services, through the Health and Labor Offices, it had not been actively used to aid in the dismantling of national armies and the building up of a vigilant international police force —on a model which the Saar election was later to prove possible. So far as the United States was concerned, any whole-hearted co-operation toward collective security was made impossible by the original premises: too many evils were still unredressed to permit stabilization. Preserving peace was one thing: protecting the *status quo* of the British, the French, or the Italian empires was quite another.

So it is useless to talk, as an editorial in the New York *Times* did, of coming back "some day," to reduction of national armaments and the institution of

98

collective security. Those were the futile halfway measures of the past. As long as military weapons may be used by any nation disposed to employ them, collective insecurity must be the result. No: when the day for peace really dawns again—whether that comes next year or at the end of the next millennium—a much more drastic contribution will be required. One cannot finally do away with war as a mode of conflict without doing away with the pretentious legal myth of unlimited national sovereignty. This means providing both the administrative and judicial services necessary for adjusting national grievances: it also means implementing the decisions of these organizations with an international police force for each continent, capable of putting down any new menace from Hitlers or Mussolinis still unborn.

As for interventionism, without even the pretense of collective security, such as might easily follow an effort to protect American property claims in China, it is an even more disastrous policy. Fighting to preserve the outposts of American finance capitalism is not a worthy aim for a democracy. Though the Open Door in China is a necessary safeguard to China's independence and an aid to world trade, it can be restored only by the institution of an Open World.

That demands a larger system of strategy than one bent upon salvaging some immediate but secondary interest in a remote territory. Indeed, it is the threat to sacrifice American lives on behalf of such humanly insignificant ends that mainly drives the mass of decent Americans into an ostrich-like pacifism. No nation in its senses today will fight for money or booty or prestige: though it may be necessary to fight for the right to exist in the face of those who desire money, booty, power and prestige. This is a fundamental distinction. No honest American policy can avoid it.

# 14. ISOLATIONISM DOES NOT GO
## FAR ENOUGH

Unfortunately, the current American policy of isolation is just as ill-founded, just as illusory, as the defunct policy of collective security. Isolationism assumes that the United States is today what England was in the nineteenth century: a tight little island. That is hardly true even now: a policy based upon this illusion will, less than ten years from now, prove a powerful aid to outside aggression.

The reason should be plain enough to convince even a congressman from the Middle West. During the last twenty years we have taken great pains, with the aid of modern technology, to break down the isolation which did indeed exist in 1920. Already transoceanic flights are common enough barely to deserve a small item in the newspapers to record them: in another decade every advanced country will have airplanes capable of making the hop without difficulty, with a margin of gas left. No army or navy man of intelligence believes that this fact opens the United

States to foreign invasion: it is indeed extremely unlikely, even if our naval defense should entirely break down, that any foreign force could be landed on our shores in sufficient numbers to do more than temporary damage.

But one must not be too easily reassured by these sensible military calculations. They unfortunately leave out a factor with which the technical mind does not sufficiently reckon—the effect of irrational forces. It is not the actual possibilities of war that count today: what leaves its mark upon the international situation is the threat of war. The worst damage that the fascists inflict is before war occurs: an imaginary damage. As a weapon for creating neurotic anxiety and paralysis of the will the airplane is without exception the most powerful instrument of warfare: the active invasion of real troops is nothing in comparison. Its value for propagandist purposes has been augmented by mythological stories of its potency, through spreading poisonous gases, and by its actual efficiency, when used by marauding fascists, in bombing and killing off women and children in unprotected centers.

Upon threat of war popular imagination, often cunningly aided by government suggestion, magnifies the possible number of enemy planes and obliterates all

102

the means of defense. The very preparations that are made to protect the civilian population—the bomb-proof shelters, the gas masks, the fire and air raid drills—only dramatize the terror and add to the partly fictitious potency of the enemy. It was the five thousand airplanes that Germany did *not* possess, added to the five thousand that they may doubtfully have had, that aided in the Berchtesgaden betrayal.

So with the fact of American immunity to military attack. The mere potentiality of German or Italian bombing squadrons, making their way to the cities of the Atlantic seaboard will, within a few years, have a *momentous political* effect. This effect will bear no relation to the amount of military damage such machines, at their luckiest, could inflict.

In short, though the United States could not be seized by a large military force, it could easily be terrorized by a small one. In this sense, the airplane has done away with geographic isolation: above all, it has done away with psychological isolation. Within the next generation the imaginary danger may indeed become an actual one, through improvements in engine design and fueling: long before that, however, its capacities for civilian demoralization will be real. The terror that gripped a multitude of radio listeners

103

in the United States at the dramatic broadcast of an invasion of the country—an invasion by imaginary creatures from Mars—demonstrates the pathological state into which fascism's brutalities have thrown the world. Our isolationism is gone. New York is actually nearer to Berlin today than it was to Philadelphia in Washington's time.

In what sense then has isolationism any meaning as a national policy? Mere withdrawal from world affairs, such withdrawal as was embodied in our Neutrality Acts, does not in the least guarantee that we will not be hurt by what goes on in other parts of the world. When American goods are cut out of a world market, that has an effect upon employment and prosperity in the factory or farm affected. When the German government strips the Jews or the Catholics of their goods and sends them forth, that fact has a natural repercussion upon our Catholic and Jewish population: indeed upon every humane citizen in the community. When the fascists rose up against the duly elected government of Spain and waged war upon it with the help of the Germans and the Italians, our attempt to isolate ourselves from this situation cost us dear. Our embargo has given power to the fascists; and the victory of fascism in Spain would

104

bring our Latin American neighbors nearer to fascism. By our obstinate belief in "neutrality" we will have aided the "peaceful" penetration of fascism into the Western hemisphere.

By its triumph in Europe fascism will become an active menace to American democracy. As interpreted by our Neutrality Acts, isolationism is nothing less than an unconditional surrender to the forces that today threaten our Constitution and our traditional way of life: indeed civilization itself. Such isolation has proved dangerous in two ways: it has given the fascists unlimited opportunity to extend their conquests, and it has given encouragement to those obscene, irrational forces in the United States that favor fascism. The fact is our isolationism does not go far enough: it denies ourselves any opportunity to influence the rest of the world, but it does not prevent the rest of the world from influencing us.

What we must isolate is not the United States but fascism. The notion that we should not lift a hand in our own defense until a troopship laden with invaders lies off Sandy Hook is as fatuous as the assumptions upon which it is based. If we wait for a military attack to take place, we will be too late to meet it with any other means than a military one. Today we have a choice of weapons to use against fascism. If we are willing to take the necessary risks that attend using them, we may be able to avoid more serious damage.

# 15. NON-INTERCOURSE—FIRST STEP

For the moment, the most serious threat to American democracy comes from that combination of passivism and pacifism by which democracies are lulled into inaction until the time for effective measures has gone by. To promote this passivism is the main effort of every fascist propagandist: they receive able if gratuitous help from liberals who are more frightened of the mere possibility of war than of the desperate actuality of fascism: likewise from pacifists who are more afraid of the munitions trust than they are of Hitler and Mussolini. The fact that most of these people are still obstinately talking about the world that existed in 1928, without apparently being aware of the fact, adds to our present handicaps.

The first requisite of a sound policy of buttressing our American democracy against fascism is that it should be capable of being put into effect immediately. This need can be met by a comprehensive Non-intercourse Act. By means of it we should cease all economic and political intercourse with the three militant fascist states that are actively threatening the world today: Germany, Italy, Japan. Specifically, such an act would consist in the following steps:

1. We should withdraw all our nationals from those countries, and with them our accredited representatives. Mr. Roosevelt's "withdrawal" of the American ambassador to Berlin in protest against the German Nazi policy of terrorism was a first step toward this end.

2. We should liquidate, as far as possible, all short and long term investments.

3. We should place a complete embargo on trade with these countries. (The fact that we have sold airplanes and munitions to both Germany and Italy during the last two years, when they were engaged in their active attempt to subdue the Spanish people, casts a sinister reflection upon our indefensible policy of withholding such materials from the Loyalist republicans in Spain.)

4. We should withhold passport privileges from citizens seeking to travel in those countries, except for scholars, churchmen, and representatives of the press: and we should prohibit the entrance of fascist nationals, with the exceptions of refugees who seek haven in the United States.

5. We should refuse entry to vessels from fascist countries even though carrying non-fascist cargoes.

6. We should begin the systematic deportation of Germans and Italians who remain fascist subjects.

7. We should withdraw the privileges of citizenship from naturalized citizens who accept the fascist doctrine of dual allegiance.

To this policy of non-intercourse with the fascist states only one large exception should be made: the free admission of fascist books, papers, and periodicals. Democracy has nothing to fear from fascist ideas. The Nazis publish no better propaganda *against* their doctrines than the little official magazine for foreign circulation, "News in Brief," in which their official acts and opinions are duly recorded.

This policy of non-intercourse has excellent historic precedent. It was invoked by Thomas Jefferson as a means of escaping the intolerable indignities which the growing supremacy of Napoleon on the European continent heaped upon countries that refused to accept his "co-ordination." That the policy worked hardship in Jefferson's day and failed to accomplish its purpose then does not mean that it would meet the same fate today. In 1806 the United States was a small insignificant seaboard power, whose abstention from trade meant little to the life of Europe. Since the hinterland of the United States was not then opened or settled, the non-intercourse policy put a crimp in domestic economics; and since a good part of the seaboard depended for its life on trade and waterborne commerce, non-intercourse put commerce as a whole at a standstill. Latin America and Asia were not alternative markets: the non-intercourse hurt the home producer and cargo-carrier without injuring Napoleon.

Today, non-intercourse would be a different matter. Our refusal to buy Japanese silk and cheapjack goods or to sell scrap-iron to Japan would put her economic activities and her war-preparations under serious handicap. Though she might still get sufficient oil from Mexico, if Mexico refused to follow our lead, the loss of a big silk customer would be felt. As far as Italy and Germany go, the immediate economic hardships we should impose upon them would be small: in the matter of trade we should even have to stand a small temporary loss. We should, however, block off the market in olive oil and wine, to the benefit of California and French producers; and we should remove Italian glass and pottery from American shelves. The fascist powers would still be able to purchase through intermediary neutral nations such of our products as they might be willing to pay for: except in the case of munitions of war, that would not harm us.

Economically, one of the most effective parts of this policy of non-intercourse would be the ruin of the cargo-carrying and tourist trade with America in German and Italian ships. Even more important would be the cutting off of tourist travel: for the exportation of American dollars by this means has been an effective aid to the German and Italian need for foreign money in what survives of their international trade. Those who are opposed to taking action of any sort against the fascist states, deliberately ignore this aspect of non-intercourse in order to minimize its economic significance.

The psychological effects of cutting off tourist travel must not be under-rated. Every year tourism sends back to this country thousands of naïve and ill-informed people, who have been duly introduced to the greatness of fascism. Many of these people visit Germany or Italy for the first time and have no basis for comparison: they regard as new fascist phenomena habits and achievements that are century-old. They come back with reports of fascist countries glow-

111

ing with prosperity, free from disorder, empty of discontent. Often they give the fascists credit for public works that were put up in Germany, for example, during the hopeful days of the Republic—mainly with the help of American capital imprudently flung into the laps of German municipalities. Such observations, such reports, are usually worthless—but by their misrepresentations they create a falsely hopeful view of fascism.

Millions of Germans and Italians naturally remain civilized human beings, courteous, kindly, helpful, even secretly sympathetic, it may be, to the persecuted minorities in their countries. This is true not because of fascism but despite fascism—in the very teeth of indoctrination and malignant lies. But the innocent tourist in Italy or Germany does what Tom Paine described in The Rights of Man: he attributes to the government in power the virtues that belong to our common humanity.

The spuriously founded good-will that fascism so cheaply creates for itself by extending to the visitor courtesies and liberties that never even momentarily belong to its own subjects would be cut off by a policy of non-intercourse. At the same time, the ill-will that fascism so assiduously propagates in democracies would be cut off, too: the embargo on travel works both ways. Fascist lecturers, fascist agents, fascist consular officials, fascist spies—and the Americas have been flooded with these people recently—would no longer have the privilege of spreading propaganda through the United States. Nor would they be able to give financial aid to organizations that seek to spread those low fears and hatreds upon which fascism lives and flourishes: anti-liberalism, anti-semitism, anti-laborism, anti-democracy.

At the present moment our relation to fascist states is entirely one-sided: to their advantage and our disablement. No American visitor in Germany or Italy or Japan is permitted to say a single word publicly on behalf of democracy or a republican system of government, or in disparagement of the Fuehrer or Il Duce or the fascist creed: to do so even in private conversation is to court arrest by the secret police. Those who do so are hustled to a railroad station in the middle of the night and promptly set on the other side of the border: even the mere tinge of these sentiments or ideas in a newspaper despatch may result in such a quick departure. A fascist in the United States, on the other hand, may raise his voice with impunity against our democracy and even criticize the

113

officers of the United States government without curtailing his stay in this country half an hour. Since there is no way of redressing this inequality by persuading the fascists to abandon censorship for free speech, and the doctrine of lèse-majesté for free criticism, a policy of non-intercourse is the only one that meets this situation.

# 16. THE HANDICAP OF DO-NOTHINGISM

Our present do-nothing policy puts democracy under a handicap. We are open to internal attack upon our institutions in a dozen forms: but we are powerless to open a counter-attack in the fascist countries. The last thing that the fascists could stand here would be a dose of their own medicine. And that is what a policy of non-intercourse would do: it would place fascism in America in precisely the state democracy occupies in fascist countries. For countries that refuse to accept the principle of mutual intercourse, the only alternative that is left to us, when they become menacing, is no intercourse at all. Such a policy preserves, unimpaired, the right of free speech and free assemblage to American citizens; but it would cut off American fascists from alien financial support and alien man-power.

One can picture sardonically the outraged howl that will go up in the fascist press throughout the world if our American democracy takes such a step to preserve its liberties. Just as the fascists, while build-

ing their war machines up to the limit of public
endurance, are always holy apostles of peace by
submission for other countries: just as they indig-
nantly denounce as war-mongers those who would
make a democratic country capable of protecting itself against their threats—so with free speech and
international intercourse. The fascists will be the first
to denounce with throaty vituperation any measure
that will lessen free-speech-for-fascists in America,
and they will castigate any blockage of the peaceful
channels of world trade at the very moment that they
comically re-assert their belief in autarchy.

The cold fact of the matter, however, is that free
speech will remain in America only so long as we
protect ourselves actively against those who would,
as the very first act of preserving their power, do
away with free speech. By holding to the abstract
principle of free speech without regard for political
reality, a doctrinaire liberalism in fact proposes to
commit suicide. So an honest person on the verge of
starvation might, by clinging to his honesty, refuse a
bottle of milk he found on a doorstep—and die. These
abstract virtues are guiding points, like the fixed
points of the compass. But neither abstract freedom
nor abstract honesty are good in themselves: they

116

are good only in so far as they create good men and promote a good society.

It is not freedom we seek but a society of free men: to preserve the man is just as important as to preserve the principle of freedom. No system of casuistry would deny the starving man the right to appropriate the bottle of milk, or would canonize as a saint the person who met his death by refusing to take it: though a sound ethics would, of course, deny him the right to rifle the silver of the man to whom the milk bottle was consigned. So with freedom of speech and movement. It is more important to preserve in America the system of relations under which men can think and exchange opinions freely and move about on their business than it is to give absolute obedience to an abstraction—until a point is reached when the whole fabric of social relations will, through this very worship of abstractions, be swept away. No political virtue is worth a cat's toenail if obedience to it wipes out the society that has generated and learned to utilize this virtue. Peace is not worth while having if its preservation enslaves or exterminates peaceful men. And no doctrine of freedom is anything but a political caricature if it leads its exponents finally to a concentration camp.

This generalization applies in fact to all the political virtues: respect for law and order, for example. In the end, the Nazis conquered Germany because the republicans stuck to the nice legal forms of government, even though they were faced with enemies who despised those forms and had threatened as soon as they achieved power to destroy them. It was not merely the timid socialists who were constrained by this respect for order: the habit was universal in every party except the Nazis. Perhaps the most pathetic spectacle of all was that of the earnest communist deputy, Torgler, who after the Reichstag had been set on fire by the Nazis, voluntarily surrendered himself to the police, that is, his enemies, in order to prove to them, that is, the people who had lighted the fire, that he had not committed the act. At the moment when he should have been organizing armed resistance to his unscrupulous opponents, he was punctiliously paying homage to the constitution they sought to abolish.

I am as well aware as my most skeptical reader that the policy of non-intercourse, hardly less than war itself, goes flat against the dearest traditions of civilized men. Every sane man believes in international intercourse; every decent person wishes to increase the linkages, social, intellectual, emotional that bind people together throughout the world. In a world that was not threatened by barbarian domination, the main effort of politics would be to remove factitious barriers and to make men at home everywhere on the planet.

But the one-way system of the fascists cannot be countered by giving the fascists the privileges of action they will not grant to people who live under democratic systems of government. With worldwide intercourse as our final goal, we must provisionally embark on a policy of non-intercourse with fascism. With a free society as our goal, we must restrict freedom to those who would destroy it. These are bitter paradoxes. Like the necessity for arming briskly against fascism, they imply a temporary defeat for our common civilization. It is only, however, by making the best of this temporary defeat that we can avoid a more permanent one: the victory of fascism.

# 17. IMPLEMENTING NON-INTERCOURSE

There is no policy that can be adopted against fascism that will not work hardship to some group. Surely the policy of doing nothing works hardship: if the extension of fascism to our Latin American neighbors cuts off American markets in that part of the world the result will be just as grievous as any that non-intercourse could introduce.

Naturally, it will be necessary to take measures to lessen immediate dislocations that will follow the imposition of non-intercourse. Alternative markets must be found for the manufacturers whose outlet is blocked by non-intercourse. Loans must be advanced to crippled industries, such as the silk textile industry, until they can take steps to meet their new situation: likewise special subventions should be given to their workers during this period. Special government aid should be given to those American residents in fascist countries who will be suddenly called upon to abandon their households and to make a fresh start in their native countries.

None of these problems is of overwhelming difficulty: but in order to lessen the immediate domestic sting of non-intercourse, we must not leave any group in the state that the New England merchants were in during the Jeffersonian period. A positive program for economic readjustments should be offered at the same time as the act itself. Private boycotts work hardship precisely because these steps are not taken.

# 18. WORKINGS OF NON-INTERCOURSE

What are the advantages of this policy of non-intercourse? The first advantage is a strategic one: it directs our national attention to the point of greatest danger, and it takes immediate action to meet it. Since the tactics of fascism are first to disintegrate and then to subjugate democracy, the policy of non-intercourse places us in a state of readiness. More than that: it puts the initiative in the hands of the world's leading democracy. Inaction, retreat, anxious waiting for the next blow to fall are demoralizing postures. How demoralizing they are the recent history of Europe gives good proof; whereas purposive action, even on a small scale, is more potent than mere armament. Even a futile gesture would be better than complete paralysis of the will; and non-intercourse is by no means a futile gesture.

So, if we have the gameness to undertake the necessary risks, we would restore to democracy throughout the world the élan, the self-confidence, the active initiative that have until now been the peculiar monopoly of the dictatorial regimes. Long in advance of any possible war, we should have struck the first blow in our own defense. That has a psychological advantage. And we should have struck our blow long before the fascist states are in a position to strike back.

Even five years from now, if the situation continues to go from bad to worse, the fascists may have the fleets of a vassal France and a Great Britain to aid them. Today, their only military strength, as against the United States, is too insignificant even to tempt an active demonstration on their part. Their press would yammer. Their dictators would snarl. But the very loudness of their response would be an indication of their temporary impotence. If we are not too oozy with fear of war to follow up our policy, the first blow would be, by the very fact that it was struck, a victory for our democracy: no mean one. And the fascist states would recognize it as such: for it would bring to their underlying population, as nothing else could, the fact that there was one powerful country in the world that was unfrightened by the bared teeth of Mussolini or by the astrological inspirations of Hitler.

Even should the fascist states respond to our non-intercourse act by declaring war their joint capacity for inflicting damage at the present time is a small one. Italy still has heavy commitments in Abyssinia and Spain. Germany, having swallowed Czechoslovakia, has still to dominate France and to wipe out the possibilities of resistance in Hungary and Poland. Japan's hands are abundantly occupied in China: occupied to the point of exhaustion. For the moment, the fascist powers have nothing to gain by declaring a war that they have not the weapons or the resources to prosecute.

By acting promptly, we shall put the Rome-Berlin-Tokyo alliance at an embarrassing disadvantage. As the months and years succeed, their relative strength will probably increase: hence the earlier we strike the more damage we do; likewise, the more time we allow for the building up of our own democratic morale and the strengthening of our own defenses. The most serious danger to be expected from a non-intercourse policy is not a *declaration* of war: we are far more likely to face undeclared acts of fascist piracy. Armed protection for American boats will abate that menace, as it did during the last years of the World War.

As a first step toward reorienting American policy

the lifting of the embargo on Spain presents itself. This embargo was sanctioned by the American government as part of its plan for co-operating with the British and French governments for preserving the peace of Europe: by now it is quite clear that it has merely given a gross advantage to the fascists, and has done nothing whatever to circumscribe or mitigate the possibility of armed conflict: quite the contrary. In point of fact, the embargo is a willful abrogation of the Treaty of 1902 with the Spanish government: a treaty that provided that a full year must take place, after due notice, before its provisions could be set aside by either party. That is a black mark against the American government. To make up for our callous morals and our false sense of expediency here, it is important that the American government not merely lift the ban upon munitions and implements of war: to rectify the ill we have done the Spanish people we should provision Republican Spain with the necessaries of life, and send them under the convoy of the American navy. To do less on behalf of those who are defending democracy there would be worse than ungenerous. Republican Spain's fight is our fight.

The policy of immediate action against fascism has many tactical advantages; and the first of them is that the time, the place, and the weapons used are of our own choosing. We do not wait for fascism to choose the right moment to strangle us, whilst we allow the forces friendly to fascism to rally together in our country and undermine our democratic morale and our will actively to resist the fascist barbarism. In using non-intercourse as our main weapon we choose an instrument that no nation in Europe could well avail itself of singlehanded: indeed, only a continental economy, like our own, could use it without serious suffering.

Again: this policy is based upon our national tradition of self-reliance: it does not involve us in blanket commitments or entangling alliances in Europe: not least, it withdraws that unseemly backing we have given the British government in its pro-fascist moves. Non-intercourse does not mean waiting for the so-called great democracies of Europe to give us a lead nor does it involve ourselves in their shifty devices for protecting their empires or their ruling classes. Non-intercourse is based primarily upon our own need for security; and to achieve it, we take the lead and follow our own line of action. The terms are ours. The aims are ours.

There is no doubt that such bold leadership would

126

rally what is left of the forces of democracy in
Europe, if they can be rallied at all. It might easily
lead to the overthrow of the pro-fascist group that now
dominates the British government: it might even lead
to more active forms of resistance against fascism,
sufficient at least to preserve the integrity of the re-
maining democratic states. What the United States
can do by way of intensified trade and adequate sup-
plies of munitions to make such resistance possible,
we should do: this applies first to Spain, then to
democratic countries like Belgium, Holland, and the
Scandinavian states: only to England and France after
their pro-fascist policy of appeasement has been aban-
doned. We should do these things, not primarily as a
means of helping Europe, but as a means of defending, with the least expenditure of overt force, our own
democracy.

Even before this book is published, so torrential
are events today, war may have broken out between
the insatiable fascist powers and one or more of their
already disillusioned appeasers. The British and
French politicians, whose generous contributions to
appeasement were at first made at other nations' expense, are somewhat dismayed to discover that they
are called upon to make equal sacrifices. If pushed too

hard, the non-fascist states may fight. Though such a war may be fought under some malodorous moral banner, it will now be empty of moral dignity. France's present "amity" toward Germany, for example, is a mere mockery. There is all the difference in the world between paying one's debts to an honest man and handing over one's money to him at the point of a gun when he has become a robber. So, too, there is a difference between opposing fascist barbarism because it is barbarous and fighting it because one's attempts at propitiating and coddling its barbarism have been perversely rejected. If war comes now it will come because the politicians of England and France have lost their chronic capacity for temporizing with aggression and palliating fraud: it will be a sign that their policy of Safety First has led the callous chauffeurs of fascism to press down on the accelerator rather than apply the brakes. (No intelligent political observer expected anything else to happen.)

But such a war will leave the United States with a serious practical problem. We will be forced, if we recognize where our own interests as a democracy lie, to help resist fascism; but at the same time, we must not entangle ourselves in a situation that is not of our making or find ourselves fighting, as in the last war, for shabby nationalist and imperialist ends that are alien, and not of our own choosing. Nevertheless, the first step toward meeting this danger involves the abandonment of our Neutrality Acts. We simply cannot be neutral toward any events that threaten to increase the scope and influence of fascism: it is not an abstract question of penalizing an aggressor state and favoring its victim: it is a practical question of lessening, for ourselves, the menace of fascism.

The Neutrality Acts and the Johnson Act stand in the way of our using the opportunity of a European war to help liquidate the fascist regimes. From the lowest standpoint possible, that of mere economy, these acts go against the present interests of the United States: like our pacifism, they are dated, in effect, 1929. No price that we can pay, by way of compounding old debts or permitting new ones to be incurred, will be anything like as heavy as the price we shall have to pay in re-armament and in loss of effective liberty if the fascist states should be victorious. From the standpoint of preserving civilization, our moral judgment against fascism must be registered, not in verbal denouncement, but in purposive acts. We cannot stay out of such a general conflict with fascism if we value our own democracy: the only question is *how, when, where,* we should step in.

But though we must abandon the shifty policy of neutrality, we must, no less, limit our commitments. In addition to the steps involved in working out our independent non-intercourse policy, our only direct military aid to the anti-fascist powers should be the use of the Navy to assist in the convoy of food and munitions. We should not let the democracies be starved out by fascist submarines; but we should exert every effort to keep our own military power intact in order that we may place our weight, at the end, on the side of a permanent organization of peace, based upon an equitable distribution of economic and political opportunities for all peoples.

While the last World War undermined the sanity of the participants for a good half dozen years or more, the new totalitarian war, a war of psychic demoralization rather than of direct military shock, will doubtless leave even more poisonous after-effects. If our immediate intervention in Europe, with ships and planes, would bring such a war to an immediate close, it would be sensible to favor it. If our keeping entirely out of the conflict would ensure the preservation of our own sanity without aiding the victory of fascism, it would be rational to favor that. Before the situation develops, one cannot make a competent judgment: all that one can provide for, in order to meet the emergency, is that our hands should not be tied. That is why an adequate policy of defense against fascism involves the repeal of our present Neutrality Acts. Fascism is a worse evil than war: that bitter truth is the foundation for any sound democratic foreign policy. Peace at any price means peace at the price of accepting fascism.

# 19. THE DOMESTIC ENEMIES
## OF DEMOCRACY

Meanwhile, the policy of non-intercourse with the aggressive fascist countries has important domestic attributes: it gives us an opportunity to cope effectively with the inimical skeleton army of fascists that already exists in the United States: spies, provocative agents, saboteurs. Plainly, no adequate policy of defense can ignore the necessity for liquidating at the earliest moment the large potential enemy that exists within our own frontiers.

These fascist sympathizers and active allies consist now of two main groups: only yesterday there were three. Probably the most dangerous of these, as we have reason to know from the activities sponsored by the notorious von Papen during the first World War are the Nazis and Nazi agents. A considerable body of Germans has already abused our hospitality, or betrayed their adopted citizenship by accepting the Nazi doctrine of identification by blood with the Third Reich. This group is busily drilling private

132

armies in various cities and spreading its gospel of anti-semitism and anti-democracy. In addition, there is a certain number of Italians who are either well-disposed toward fascism or openly in favor of adopting its methods. Both these groups are actively abetted by their consular representatives.

There is no way of accurately estimating the numbers of these foreign fascists; for plainly, there is a large body of Germans and Italians, to say nothing of German-Americans and Italo-Americans who are as vehemently opposed to fascist despotism as a Jefferson or a Lincoln would be. It is not the country of origin that ranges a person as an enemy of democracy: it is his active present attitude toward fascism: his desire to further the general policy of repression and reprisal followed by fascist governments.

Up to a little while ago these foreign elements had a powerful ally: the Roman Catholic hierarchy. While the great body of Catholics in America are genuinely loyal to the institutions of democracy, despite their authoritarian Church, the Church itself, in recent years, for long chose to ally itself with democracy's chief enemy, fascism. The Catholic priesthood even took over the typical fascist hoax of making war on popular government by playing up the

133

factitious threat of communism, and by branding plain liberal reform as an active contribution to bolshevism. In a country as overwhelmingly unbolshevik as the United States, that was a particularly odious move: all the more indefensible because, since 1930, Soviet Communism has been on the defensive: indeed, ever since 1920 it has not made a single conquest of any country.

As for the popular notion that fascism has come into existence as a bulwark against communism, the facts are plain. Where has communism made its smallest gains? In the United States and Great Britain, the two countries that have the oldest and surest forms of democratic government. The ebbing of official communism has not been due to the "protection" offered by fascism: on the contrary, *in so far as the method of communist dictatorship has had any effective influence in Europe it has been through the very agency of fascism.* For Mussolini himself has acknowledged that fascism deliberately patterned its political methods on those of the Russian dictatorship: fascism took over the ruthlessness that had always been characteristic of despotic rule in Russia: likewise it took over the totalitarian state and the supremacy of a single party.

134

In other words, fascism copied zealously from the communist dictatorship precisely those elements that have made it impossible for a believer in democracy to give assent to the methods whereby the communist party bureaucracy had, with the aid of an army and an extra-constitutional secret service, maintained their supremacy in Russia. The sinister features of communism are not communist at all but Russian: it is these features that have been actively incorporated in the governments which maintain their terroristic hold on Hitler's Germany and Mussolini's Italy. The fascists have indeed rejected for the most part the humane, enlightened purposes of communism: those in which many good men in every age have believed, from Plato to Saint Thomas More: from Campanella to Abraham Lincoln. It was only the ancient Russian tradition of barbarous violence and systematic repression that served the fascist aims.

Hence the Christian religion, so far from being protected against inimical atheistic forces by fascism, actually puts itself in the hands of such forces in any alliance with fascism. State worship and vulgar deification of the Leader are the principal forms of fascist religion; and the typical fascist virtues savagely exclude the virtues of Christianity: gentleness, mercy, charity, peace. In a strict theological sense, the concept of the Leader is that of antichrist. The spiritual humiliation of the papacy through its concord with Mussolini, and its outright persecution and denigration under the Nazis, should have taught Rome—and the rest of the Christian world—a swift lesson. But apparently certain underlying reactionary forces in the Church refused to profit by that experience until the persecutions and cruelties practiced by the fascists had reached mountainous proportions.

Our American government is founded on the deliberate separation of Church and State. On these terms organized religion, and in particular that of the Catholics, has flourished here as nowhere else during the last century. Despite this fact, the hierarchy in America, with a few brave exceptions, has until very recently been outspoken in behalf of the fascists. Popular charlatans within the Church, like the lie-quoting Father Coughlin, have by word of mouth and in print allied themselves to those reactionary forces in Europe which are bent on the extirpation of democracy: to come upon anti-semitism and pro-fascism in its full-blown European form one must read Father Coughlin's weekly, "Social Justice." Since the utterances of an ordained priest are not those of an irresponsible private individual, the Church cannot escape censure for permitting his well-poisoned fascist rat-bait from being offered to the faithful throughout the country as pious food.

Today, the best friends of the Catholic Church are those liberal elements within it who are as keenly aware as any non-member that the policy of bombing defenseless villages in Spain is not hallowed by the fact that the bomb is released by a flier who has received the blessing of his Bishop, or by the fact that the bomb itself may fall on the cradle of an unbaptized child. These people know that the commonplaces of social reform in democratic Europe, measures heartily supported by the Catholic Welfare Council, do not become communistic menaces because they are applied in America. They know, too, that a victory for the unspeakable Franco in Spain is not a victory for Christianity; nor even, in the long run, for the Church of Rome. Such humane minds—a George Shuster or a Monsignor Ryan—do much to offset those whose unreal mouthings against the communists are a cloak for the reactionary wing within the Church.

Plainly it is not communism that menaces the peace of the Church in democratic America: it is its own strange outbursts of hysterical intolerance. There are

137

ancient reasons for this hysteria in countries like Spain: among other things, a guilty past. But there are no true reasons in America; for such discriminations as the Church has suffered from here do not come from liberal movements but from reactionary ones: the Ku Klux Klan, for example. The Church has been threatened by nothing in America except its own folly. By actively siding with the fascists it has been arming its enemies and putting into the opposite camp those who, by their very love for democracy and liberty, are its best protectors.

Fortunately, the pitiable sufferings of the Catholics in Germany, abetted by Mussolini's farcical attempt to align his "racial" policy with that of Hitler's, have belatedly caused a change of heart in the higher officers of the Church. The number of prelates who have taken an open stand against fascist barbarism has increased: the belief in democracy, according to recent plans, will be made a positive element in Catholic school instruction. These are all happy signs. The Church has much political evil to undo: but if its about-face prove permanent and widespread our American democracy may well be thankful to the cold-blooded maniacs in fascist Europe who have helped bring the change about.

138

Against the second fascist group in America, that of intransigent industrialists who seek to maintain the absolutism of their rule, as practiced anciently in the company town, the policy of non-intercourse would also partly operate. Such anti-democratic methods as they practice and advocate would constitute a weakening of our democratic front: they would be subject to a popular pressure that does not exist when the country is in a less militant state. Our stone-age industrialists have, without knowing the ideology, been brought up on the Hitlerian principle of leadership. Instead of accepting their workers as responsible participators and intelligent co-operators in the work, they have demanded unconditional obedience on the worker's part and irresponsibility on their own. The Wagner Labor Act is one of the most powerful democratic weapons that has been produced in this country: an end to one-sided and arbitrary rule in industry. It needs to be strengthened rather than renounced. Our more progressive industries, led by men who have claims to industrial statesmanship, have in principle accepted the need for democratic participation and security of livelihood.

So, too, the Social Security Act and the W.P.A., the latter by giving immediate relief without forfeiting the individual's self-respect, and the former by promising to safeguard the industrial worker against the caprices of fortune, have lifted that state of desperation which prompts men to accept the slavery of fascism and vent their wrath upon its scapegoats. A permanent public works program, planned in advance of dislocations and depressions, is the first line defense against fascism.

By excluding foreign fascist propaganda and by creating a popular movement against fascism, non-intercourse would aid in bringing the less enlightened kind of employer to book. Anti-laborite industrial leaders, providers of chemical and propagandist poison gas, promoters of organized lawlessness, would finally be brought into line: or at least driven to cover. Any effort to foster fascism by devious support to fascist organizations and agents would come pretty close to treason: close enough perhaps to make reactionary industrialists think twice before dipping into their purses. This holds, too, for the extra-legal activities of native fascist organizations like the original Ku Klux Klan and its more recent imitators, such as the Silver Shirts. Deprived of uniforms, foreign aid, and corrupt political tolerance, they would wilt.

In short, non-intercourse would deprive domestic

fascist groups of active external support and direction from abroad: it would isolate them: it would brand them as enemies of our democracy: and in the very act of singling them out it would help put a curb on their activities. But such indirect means of halting domestic fascism are not enough. As a matter of elementary military protection, the national registration and surveillance of all active fascists should be undertaken. Likewise it is imperative at once to disband all private armies: including extra-governmental cadet corps. Uniforms, again, should be prohibited to all private bodies, except workers who need identification in their work. This would lessen the opportunities for organized disruption and it would reserve military force for the duly constituted arms of the government, sworn to respect and uphold the Constitution and the laws of the United States.

One final threat must also be dealt with as a matter of domestic policy. In cases where the laws of the United States and the safeguard of the Bill of Rights have been suspended by a local fascist organization— as happened originally in Louisiana under Huey Long and has come about again in Jersey City under Mayor Hague—the President of the United States should be specifically empowered by the Congress to

141

declare a state of emergency, and to restore, under martial law, the regular processes of constitutional American government: secret ballot, multi-party elections, an independent judiciary, and so forth.

Doubtless the President already has such a power if the emergency seems to him grave enough: but the passage of a law to this effect should reinforce his nominal power and in some degree make it mandatory. It was only the timely murder of Huey Long that prevented a grave national situation from arising in Louisiana: perhaps later in the whole country. Just because our loose federal organization gives the opportunity for such anomalies to exist, our democracy needs some additional measure of protection against their menace. We should not have to rely upon the independent judgment of a beneficent assassin to accomplish an end which may be easily consummated by more orderly methods. Patches of fascism are like focal points of infection: they may transmit their poison to the whole political organism. Timely cauterization is indicated, if we are to preserve the health of the democratic body politic.

# 20. RE-FORTIFICATION OF DEMOCRACY

The internal reconstruction of our democratic polity to meet the menace of fascism is no less important than the adoption of a militant foreign policy. Indeed, one hinges on the other. If I have emphasized the foreign aspect more, it is partly because the current defense of the more liberal do-nothing group is that fascism is purely a domestic phenomenon, and that if we clean house in America we need make no more active contribution to our own defense. The history of Europe and Asia this last ten years proves that this apology for inaction is based on pious hopes and feeble illusions. People who are too prudent to fight at all will not have the courage to fight domestic fascism.

Certain necessary steps for establishing a sound political and industrial order on lines that do not violate our ultimate democratic principles have been admirably outlined by Dr. Max Lerner. I heartily recommend his thoughtful and pregnant suggestions, embodied in "It is Later Than You Think." The existence of his book enables me to shorten the present argument.

In doing this, I do not forget that it is only by comparison with totalitarian countries that democracy may be said to flourish in America. I do not underestimate the weaknesses that a century and a half of self-government have disclosed: the prevalence of mediocrity in our state and national legislatures; the distrust of trained intelligence and high culture; the autocratic and arbitrary methods of industrial management; the dogged inertia of most organized labor; our failure, once free land had disappeared, to safeguard political equality with economic opportunity. Nor do I fail to realize the existence of more fascist counter-currents. Though the presidential election of 1936 lessened the fear of undue control of public opinion by an irresponsible capitalist press, it did not remove the dangers of more subtle forms of propaganda and indoctrination by those who hold financial power. Finally, I do not forget that the treatment of minorities in America, above all the treatment of the Indian and the Negro, has pages that have been as black as any that the fascists have written. Our country is not spotless: but that is quite a different thing from saying

144

that, like the Rome-Berlin axis, it has made an official cult of dirt.

By long tradition, America is overwhelmingly democratic: it has been always ready, as Whitman urged, to rise against the never-ending audacity of elected persons. There is one item, however, that will be the proof of our government's sense of democratic responsibility in meeting the menace of fascism: that is in the policy that is framed to meet our military needs. No one who has followed this plea for a militant democracy can believe that I propose to sacrifice democracy in order to obtain militancy. But at the present moment this is one of the dangers that seriously confronts us: unless our government takes positive steps to reorient its present defense program, it will break down our democratic front and seriously weaken the popular resistance to fascism.

Perhaps the most grievous mistake that was made by the Wilson government at the beginning of 1917 was in the institution of what was glibly called universal service: in other words, military conscription. This not merely placed an unusable amount of manpower at the command of an army that was incapable of handling it adequately under limitations of time, equipment, and organization: it removed the great safeguard of democracy against senseless and unpopular war: the right of voluntary enlistment.

The acceptance of conscription as a first step in war, rather than as a last desperate resort, has probably done more than any other act to make war deeply unpopular in America, no matter what the circumstances our country confronts. This notion of completely mobilizing man-power for active service is a totalitarian conception of war: but unfortunately embodied in the army's program for M-Day. As long as our military organization commits the country to such plans, so long will there be a just suspicion that the object of this mobilization is to achieve a fascist control over the lives, the property, the working power, and the opinions of the American people. In order to make this totalitarian act palatable, our politicians have had to make such abortive compromises with public opinion as our neutrality policy, coupled with promises never to use the army outside the country. It was, indeed, only by vigorous administration pressure that the proposal for a popular plebiscite on war was rejected: a proposal that would handicap democracy's resistance to fascism even more viciously than the Neutrality Acts.

Now it happens that no actual danger of invasion

146

with which the American people may be confronted during the next dozen years would justify the existence of an army of more than five or six hundred thousand men at the outside. To bring that force to the highest pitch of excellence it should contain two kinds of people: those who have chosen arms as a profession and those who enlist temporarily because they are zealously concerned to protect the institutions of their country. An army of that high caliber can be achieved only by voluntary enlistment. To serve in such an army should be an honor: zeal, enthusiasm, intensity of interest, applied intelligence are what are demanded—not grudging routine. Such an army must be supported by free workers: not by conscripts. To keep both military and production levels high, the maximum opportunity for free service, willingly rendered, should be secured. Convict labor is not a guarantee of efficiency any more than unwilling conscript service ensures martial valor.

The proper role of the American army, during the next generation, will be that of protecting the American people against fascism: it cannot be fulfilled by turning our democracy into a counterpart of fascism —even for duration of war. If the principles of democracy are respected, the necessary interest and en-

147

thusiasm for maintaining fighting efficiency will generate itself: behind the lines no less than at the front. And if voluntary service is substituted for conscription, our foreign policy need not be bound by its present limitation: that nothing at all can be done effectively in our defense unless we move the reckless gigantic juggernaut of wholesale military mobilization. To accept conscription before there is an active need for it, is to lose the war to fascism before we have even struck a blow.

There is still another reason for insisting upon the need for voluntary service. We must deliberately seek to attract into the army and navy minds of a higher order of intelligence than have usually gone into the martial occupations. We must make up for limited man-power by effective intelligence and a high order of technical skill, as well as zealous spirit. The stultification of military effort by the existing bureaucracy is a handicap that no democratic government should tolerate: hence we must alter West Point's sterile discipline and parrotlike mode of learning, which either cripples good minds or disgusts them with army service. Parade ground regimentation and pass-the-buck efficiency must go: an American army and navy must handle a complex series of moves without con-

148

fusion or indecision: the powers of autonomous action must be kept high in every branch of the service and in every rating. This is precisely where democracy, by its very belief in the intelligence and by its practical sagacity, will have the edge in any fight with the fascists.

In short, if our democracy is to become militant, our army must in compensation be civilianized: it must not become an old maid's home for those who are incompetent to face the competitions and uncertainties of civilian life.

The removal of the fascist specter of wholesale conscription is the first sane move that our government must make if it is honestly concerned to protect democracy in America. If it does so, it will have no difficulty in getting co-operation on a positive program of re-armament that will make us capable of dealing effectively, now or later, with the venomous hostility of the fascist states.

Mark that I make no effort to gloze in purely pacifist terms the assumptions of a non-intercourse policy. Force is the sole argument that the fascist worshipers of force understand—and cringe before. Good intentions, amiable programs, helpful admonitions, civilized warnings, pious remonstrances, tactful avoidance of offense, are all useless in dealing with the fascist mentality unless they are backed by indisputable physical power. The only way whereby the fascists can be prevented, ultimately, from attacking our American democracy, or at least attempting to terrorize it into submission, is by creating an army, a navy, and an air force that will make it unwholesome for them to commit piracy and impossible for them to launch with any prospect of success a full-scale attack.

An active policy against fascism is an uphill policy. It is difficult: it demands sacrifices: it carries risks. None of the risks and burdens is ultimately as great as those which a policy of passive inaction would surely bring on; but they are not inconsiderable. The very attention that we must give to fascism will distract us from humanly more significant matters: no country can manufacture the necessary weapons of military defense without wantonly spending to this end capital that should go into the building of workers' houses, the re-building of cities, to furthering the processes of education and culture. Fascism gives us an exacerbating choice: it makes us waste our efforts upon barbarous processes whose only rational purpose is protection against barbarism. So, too, we must divert into the study of warfare some of the best minds of the younger generation: another painful sacrifice.

There is no honest way of making these measures attractive. For war, the very possibility of war, is hateful to civilized man. The policy of non-intercourse, and the positive effort needed to implement our resistance to fascism with due military means, are not in any sense *desirable:* the fact remains that they are necessary. The axiom on which this policy is based is that fascism has already declared war upon democracy and that its victories in Europe and Asia, as they roll up energy and aggressiveness, will threaten every other part of the world. If we must finally fight, we will fight only as a last resort, seizing a reluctant alternative to something far more brutal and disastrous than war itself—the universal reign of fascism.

Do not fancy that we can secure peace on more agreeable terms. The nightmare that now confronts us will not disappear if we close our eyes tightly and smile propitiatory smiles: that is the behavior of children. Unfortunately, the present world is not fit for children to live in: fascists delight to drop bombs on their innocent heads: such exercises give the loyal fascist a peculiar aura of virility, which has the unique physical property of being visible only to the fascist

151

eye. It may be that fascism will continue to spread only as long as children are weak: fascism lives on easy victories and may be stunned by a single big defeat: perhaps permanently vanquished.

At all events, we must put aside our childish credulity about the possibility of civilizing the fascists: the policy of appeasement makes the lion stronger: it does not remove his teeth or lessen his ferocity. The behavior of the German Nazis after their galling triumph in Czechoslovakia has brought this home to almost everyone in the world except those who made that triumph possible. Likewise we must throw off our cynical disbelief as to the possibility of democracy's resisting fascism: for two years the brave Spanish Loyalists have shown us that the impossible can be accomplished in the face of handicaps a thousand times more serious than those the United States must face. If we do not wish to become ghosts, we must take on the tasks of men: *men must act.*

And it is only by positive action that democratic countries will fortify their own morale: this is far more important, as I have pointed out before, than the merely mechanical protection afforded by armaments. The main thing to remember is that fascism's victories, always and everywhere, have not been based upon either an absolute command of domestic majorities or upon the superiority of fascist arms and military leadership. The fascist principle is to bully and blackmail the indecisive: to fight only the weak: to conquer with exemplary frightfulness the helpless. Fascism's main strength lies in its capacity for demoralization. The best way for a country to acquire the courage necessary to resist fascism is to take the first steps to resist it. Inaction, neutrality, retreat: these are fascisms' allies. Let our cagey counselors of weak-kneed passivity, like Senator Borah and his followers, remember this. What democracy needs is a state of what Thomas Mann calls "soldierly readiness." Our greatest safeguard will be the fascists' knowledge that we are ready to fight. This applies to the domestic enemy no less than the foreign one. In a tight place, democracy is worth dying for.

# 21. PASSIVISM AND APPEASEMENT

The opposition to taking any positive steps to defend our own democracy is based on various grounds. The main argument is that it is dangerous; for it may bring on war. I think I have answered this. Danger is an inescapable part of the present situation, as it would be in a menagerie if the lions, the tigers, and the rattlesnakes had gotten loose. We shall not avert the danger by shrinking into a corner. We must confront it like men.

Perhaps the argument for passivism that goes home straightest to the common-sense American is that the United States spent thousands of lives and billions of dollars to save the world for democracy between 1917 and 1919. And what came of the effort? Little was gained by the war toward creating the necessary framework in public law and international administration for a state of peace: democracy, so far from being saved, was eventually thrown to the dogs. But we must not be confused by these pitiful results. What was wrong was not that we sought to preserve de-

154

mocracy: what alone was wrong was that we failed.

In their legitimate skepticism over much of the hysterical apologetics for war, which assumed that the British Empire was run by Galahads, many people have come to accept the economic interpretation of our actions as one that in fact explains them. According to this fable, the war was entered into by the United States to save the Morgan loans to the Allies: the whole effort was the result of a plot between the bankers, the munitions makers, and the foreign imperialists: hence presumably it is the same lot of people who alone seek to work up resistance to fascism now.

Undoubtedly all these interests wanted the Allies, who were their customers, to win; undoubtedly they did their best to embroil the United States. But to seek in this the public motive for the war is like saying that the only reason one has for traveling from New York to Washington is to get the railroads out of their financial difficulties. What made millions of intelligent Americans join hands with such rascals and profiteers is that something else actually was at stake. Why, toward the end of the war, did the higher type of German—I have met many—fervently wish the Allies to win? It was because the peace of Versailles, though a monstrosity, was incomparably saner and humaner than anything that the Germans would have made had they been victorious.

And mark this: something was actually gained by America's entrance into the war on behalf of democracy: a breathing space. Germany's assault on democracy was staved off for another twenty years. Lack of good-will and intelligence, the positive presence of imperialistic greed, capitalist desire to dominate the workers, and upper-class fear of needed socialization all prevented this breathing spell of twenty years from being a permanent victory for democracy: but it was certainly better than immediate serfdom as vassals of a triumphant, militaristic, still essentially feudal Germany. That we did not gather the beneficent results of a democratic victory is not a proof of the notion that we were fooled or misguided when we sought to save democracy.

There is, however, still another specious argument that the passivists make. This consists in the notion that the United States has sufficient resources to do without the rest of the world: by striving after self-sufficiency we shall achieve safety. We will not meddle with the outside world, and the outside world will therefore have no excuse to meddle with us.

From a political standpoint, this argument pre-

156

supposes a pre-fascist world, in which conquest had ceased to be an acceptable element in state policy: it assumes that the fascist states will in future breathe a spirit of pacifism like that which England gave public expression to during the Baldwin regime. To continue to maintain this notion in the present situation is extremely ingenuous: not to say simple-minded. But the argument in fact assumes an artless confidence about the prospects of fascism because it has underlying sympathies with its system of ideas: it is a sort of antiseptic and surgical fascism: fascism without its characteristic stench, violence, butchery, and terror.

One of the best expressions of this point of view is that of Mr. Jerome Frank, who at least extends his concept of autarchy to cover the Western hemisphere, rather than the United States. The assumption taken by this kind of isolationist is that war arises only out of a conflict of economic interests. By withdrawing economic hostages from Europe and Asia we shall therefore be withdrawing the sole occasion for war.

If democracy could be safeguarded so easily, the method would be admirable. But the very grounds of the argument demolish the effectiveness of the superstructure.

For the advocates of autarchy casually assume

that the autarchic nations of Europe will remain satisfied to exist in their self-imposed shell. The fact is that this shell has been built up temporarily for purely military purposes: it demands day-by-day sacrifices that less terrorized populations accept with docility only under the extreme pressure of war. Once Germany and Italy are in a position where they can no longer, by any coalition of powers, be starved out—and they have almost reached that point now—the next step is expansion. The move toward Germany's expansion has already taken place in Central Europe, as well as in her preliminary demands for colonies: similarly Italy, having achieved the barren conquest of Abyssinia, has begun to cry for Tunisia, for Corsica, even for Nice.

For states that have set irrational ends as their goals, autarchy is an elastic term. The fascists claim supremacy over all inferior, non-military, non-Aryan peoples. Is it conceivable, then, that they will accept a permanent disparity of resources, and not claim a better living for their compatriots through booty and perquisites than the democratic nations are able to achieve by production and trade? Already Germany has tentacles in Brazil: so has Italy in Argentina. If Italy and Germany should succeed in converting the peninsula of Spain into a fascist stronghold—and nothing except a bold democratic countermarch can prevent it—their next move will be to divide up Latin America.

That fascist domination need not take place by actual invasion: the new method of conquest is both more brutal and more subtle than the old-fashioned kind; for it depends upon first erecting a fascist Trojan horse in each of the countries over which it seeks supremacy. But what becomes of a policy of autarchy for the Western hemisphere once this move is taken? Would any amount of strained self-sufficiency prevent a conflict between the United States and the wielders of fascist power in the Latin American states? The policy of retreating further into our shell would only bring us closer to fascism: the reduction in our standard of living, the acceptance of substitute goods, the existence of a permanent economic crisis, a paralyzing sense of inferiority and insecurity: in short, the very broth in which the germs of active fascism mightily multiply.

It is no answer to these suppositions to say that they are wild: fascism is wild. It is the very pathology of fascism that makes these developments likely. In a rational world there would be no obstacles whatever to worldwide trade and worldwide intercourse: there would be no occasion for armaments or even for embittered economic conflicts. For it is easy to prove in sensible terms of gain and loss that none of these measures pays: economic justice is the highest form of expediency and the most practical sort of politics. Norman Angell demonstrated this once and for all in "The Great Illusion": but his demonstration was not heeded, though his proofs were, and still are, sound.

In other words, no policy of hard-boiled isolationism will prevent the United States from running afoul of the fascists' need for expansion. As long as democracy persists in the United States, we shall be a menace to fascism: a serious potential enemy. Theoretically each state in the world today might become a self-contained system, if it were content to accept permanently the low standard of living that would result, but that theoretic possibility would not ensure against rivalry and conflict and conquest unless each state had identical resources, identical opportunities, and parallel political purposes as states.

This is not, I repeat, to accept the specious fascist division of the world into the haves and the have-nots. So long as goods are permitted to cross national boundaries the only have-not nations are those lacking

160

in collective knowledge and skill. It is solely the desire for self-sufficiency that makes Germany, for example, a have-not nation today: before the war, when she competed in world markets with the rest of the world, Germany was a highly prosperous industrial country: one of the great "haves." But under an autarchic economy the difference between the haves and have-nots is real: it is the fundamental difference that the economist describes under the law of rent: inequalities in soils, in mineral resources, in wind and water and sun power.

Mark the inevitable result. Autarchy, so far from curbing the tendency toward physical territorial expansion, will probably only increase it: autarchic nations will seek to accomplish by political means—namely, territorial seizure or feudal vassalage—what peoples hitherto accomplished by the methods of trade. With each new appeasement, this tendency will become more marked. Expansion will take place only in a secondary way through trade: the greater part of it will be tribute, plunder. In the fascist theology, tribute and plunder are rewards for military virtue. Once the "commanding" race gets the habit of living at the expense of the slave peoples it has conquered that habit will deepen. The predatory type of organization will

161

give way to a parasitic type. First the vulture's beak: then the tapeworm.

So much then for the gullible notion of the isolationist that American autarchy, or continental self-sufficiency, will ensure our peaceful existence. The meek willingness of the sheep not to compete with the lion for prey does not ensure the sheep against the lion's attack. To isolate our country from multifold co-operation with the rest of the world is to weaken us: our intellectual and moral strength, no less than our physical strength, is in proportion to the number of ties that bind us to the rest of humanity. A person who is only an American is only half a man: indeed only half an American. What we must isolate, let me stress again, is not our own democracy but fascism.

## 22. DEMOCRACY MUST DARE!

If the fascist states continue their policy of conquest without halting or breaking down, the role of the United States is plain. Eventually we are destined to play the part of Byzantium during the Dark Ages in Europe: a beleaguered island of culture and civilization amid the rising sea of barbarism.

There are various ways in which we can mitigate the dangers of this situation. Perhaps the greatest handicap we must overcome is that of a stable population; for we can feed and clothe and equip and nurture many more people than the maximum that will be reached around 1955. If we are to find allies to carry on the single-handed fight upon barbarism that may finally be forced on us, we must not overlook the opportunity to gather them directly into our fold. This indicates the need for a reversal of policy and sentiment along two lines: an immediate change in our immigration laws, and an eventual re-orientation of custom and belief in the realm of family life —if our Byzantine role actually develops.

163

The basis of our present immigration policy is one of the least defensible things in our public law: equaled perhaps only by the denial of the vote in the South to the Negro. Our existing immigration law deliberately discriminates between the immigrants on the fascist basis of "race." Thanks to the pseudo-science preached by people like Madison Grant and Lothrop Stoddard, and translated into popular lingo by the yellow journals, our Congress in 1924 adopted an immigration policy which placed a premium upon people coming from the so-called nordic stocks. It restricted immigration to fixed quotas without reference to rate of assimilation or need.

The whole basis of this discrimination was superstitious. It assumed either that a single country like Germany held only a single race, or that a single culture-pattern, like that of the Germans', was closer to that of the United States than the culture-pattern of an Italian or Russian: although the plain fact is that the deeply servile political habits of many Germans may be a serious impediment to their citizenship in a free democracy. Our whole concept of immigrant-preference is so viciously false to facts that it is not surprising to find that it won the open approbation of Hitler, in Mein Kampf: it indeed formed a pattern

164

for his further perversions on behalf of an entirely mythical creature called the Aryan.

Now, the slowing up of population increase throughout the world has reduced the natural pressure of immigration, quite apart from the slackening of economic opportunities in America or the deliberate discouragement of emigration in European states. But it is still true that our discriminatory policy has no rational basis: neither has the size of the present quotas. Today the course of circumstances offers us the most desirable kind of immigrant: the victims of fascist persecution. These mostly are the humane people, the intelligent people, the democratic people in every country that has submitted to fascism: they include, among others, the very cream of Europe's intelligentsia.

More and more such people are knocking at our gates: presently Czechoslovakia, possibly France, almost certainly Spain will send their quotas too. The belief in democracy, which these people for the most part share, makes them the most desirable candidates for American citizenship. Forced to migrate, they have already part of the equipment of pioneers. With intelligent public aid they could be distributed to just those parts of the country where their abilities and skills could be most fully used. There are regions like the Northwest, well-endowed with resources, that are lonely for men: here is the seat of a new effort in city building and regional development, provided we can supply a well-assorted cultural group, capable in time of mastering the life and raising civilization there to an even higher level.

For our own security, no less than to succor the unfortunate—which is also a duty—our immigration policy should be entirely revised. It should place a strict barrier against immigrants from fascist countries who would still keep their allegiance to the totalitarian dictatorships: it should, on the other hand, offer special facilities to those refugees from fascist barbarity who seek to make a fresh start in the New World. A large colonization loan, and a Resettlement Administration on the lines of that but lately disbanded, are indicated.

These measures are no less important than an enlargement and revision of quotas. For us to deplore the merciless fascist persecutions of their unwanted subjects without taking prompt steps to provide asylum for the refugees is empty sentimentalism. The world's disorder imposes great tasks and difficult sacrifices upon our country. We must accept these demands if we are to preserve our self-respect as Americans.

The chief obstacle toward this revision of public policy is the notion that every new addition to the population is a potential addition to the unemployed: according to this ignorant view, the newcomers take away jobs from those already here. This is the basis for labor's opposition to immigration. The fallacy consists in confusing the population problem with the economic problem. Until industry has found a stable basis for production in a series of measures that permits rising productivity without a falling income, unemployment will continue to exist even were the population halved: it would become relatively no more serious were it doubled.

If an excess of workers were responsible for industry's present crisis, it would be hard to explain why the period that gave the United States its maximum rate of population-increase by immigration has always been accepted as one of relative prosperity. Indeed, one may justify the lowering of immigration barriers by this fact: our industry was keyed during the last century for an expanding population; and one of the most important things that has caused an increase in unemployment has been the falling off of demand

167

without any provision being made for a co-ordinate shrinkage in plant, equipment, capitalization—or alternatively, of meeting the horizontal contraction of the market by an equivalent vertical rise in the individual's standard of living. *An increased immigration at the present moment would serve as a cushion to soften the blow, until we had taken other permanent measures to meet the approaching stability of population.*

At all events, population-increase does not become an economic problem until a given area has reached the saturation point. For the United States as a whole, this point is still a long way off. The way to take care of unemployment is by revamping our economic system, not by decreasing the number of people who live in the United States. When the production-consumption cycle is in order, every new citizen who is added to the country increases its wealth by his very presence. Eventually, the bread we cast upon the waters will come back to us, according to the biblical promise.

Against the spinsterly policy of withdrawal and shrinkage all along the line—withdrawal from world affairs, withdrawal from multifold economic relations, withdrawal of population—I advocate just the opposite policy: that of expanding and intensifying all our efforts on behalf of a high human culture. If the fascist sword is to be kept from dominating the world, it will not be because we have put our faith in umbrellas and overshoes, even though they are of American manufacture. We must multiply our democratic numbers: we must take on new responsibilities. Our democracy must not cringe and cower: we must take command: we must will our new destiny into existence. Intensity of living, rather than mere prolongation of life: an eager fertility rather than the prudent avoidances and attenuated desires of the middle-aged are the supports of the good life. The weak, the anemic, the tepid, the all-too-prudent are not the sort who can make a stand against a barbarian onslaught.

Each outburst of fresh energy on behalf of civilization and democracy will fortify our capacities and make us more capable of maintaining the precious values to which all humanity is heir. Each good that we relinquish will only make us weaker: each timorous inhibition we impose upon ourselves will only make us more unsure: each retreat will only make us less capable of holding on to the poor remnant that we still possess. Isolationism is another word for desolationism. It is the free-moving creatures, above all the most unprotected and active of them, not the armored reptiles, that have inherited the world.

Successfully to oppose the barbarian forces that now threaten us, democracy must dare to take the initiative. There is no safety for the living in merely avoiding death: the only effective means of preserving life is to beget it and nurture it and pursue it more intensively. This holds for both the things of the body and the things of the spirit.

George Russell (A.E.) once said that a man becomes the image of the thing he hates. That warning must be kept in mind as we buckle down to the task of holding fascism at bay. To keep fascism from imprinting us with its image, we must not resort solely to measures of opposition: our safety lies in a more positive and passionate commitment to the needs of civilization. When human energies are low, nothing seems worth the effort: when they are keyed high and poured into constructive tasks they gain in strength by their very expenditure: the more we demand of ourselves, the fuller will be the response we shall get from our environment.

But we shall not achieve the necessary élan merely by comfortably holding out the prospect of a few extra hours to dawdle in or a few extra comforts to ease the busy grind, as democracy's highest reward. No one was ever moved to a mighty effort by the prospect of a suburban cottage and a safe job. There must be equity and justice in our economic life, not simply because an "economy of abundance" makes this easy; but because equity and justice are conditions for our spiritual health, whilst greed, class-exploitation, and callousness are signs of deep-seated social ailments. And so in every department of our life: unless the active *will-to-create* be present, we shall achieve neither security nor a society that is worth the effort needed to safeguard it.

There is no creation without travail and sacrifice. To preserve our civilization, we must be ready to give the world more than we get: the nation or the individual who looks for tangible returns and quick profits will be the very one who will come back empty-handed. Democracy cannot flourish on half-hearted, divided efforts: we must exact the impossible of ourselves if we are to achieve the best that is possible out of the present situation. That which the soldier gives with quiet desperation on the field of battle must become the commonplace gift of the day: every mechanic, every clerk, every farmer, every house-

171

wife, writer, scientist, artist, inventor, industrialist, business man must dedicate himself to the larger task of upholding our democratic civilization: this, before he permits himself a second thought about his individual fortunes. Only on such terms, in an hour as threatening as the present one is, can our permanent human heritage be saved.

Whatever our generation may seek by way of fulfillment, it cannot hope for a relaxed, a sheltered, or an easy life. Sacrifice: hard discipline: soldierlike devotion to duty at any cost of comfort or convenience —these are the conditions that life imposes upon us if we are to escape the degradations and the brutalities that fascism seeks to make once more the common lot of mankind. "Allons!" as Whitman cried, "through struggles and wars! The goal that was named cannot be countermanded." Struggle and war are our portion: even for those of us who know most fully the uses of peace. But our gravest task is to resist the fascist barbarian's dynamic will-to-destruction. By defining the issues of our struggle, by projecting our purposes clearly, we may transform the character of our war. Beyond this dark conflict with barbarism we may hope to emerge—again in Walt

Whitman's words—into a humaner order, an order of *"saner wars—sweet wars—life-giving wars."* The goal cannot be countermanded; but the conditions for achieving it are inexorable: *men must act.*